# Diabetic Delights:

## Flavorful Recipes for Healthy Living | Nourish Your Body, Nurture Your Health

Marigold Finch

# Table of Contents

# Introduction

Our physical health often takes a back seat to our hectic daily lives. Our everyday tasks are like a never-ending balancing act, and there are a lot of deadlines and family commitments that we have to attend to. Still, our bodies bear the brunt of it all, and for some of us, diabetes is the shape that this brunt takes.

Imagine yourself smack dab in the midst of a bustling coffee shop, where the aroma of home-brewed coffee fills the air. There are a plethora of appetizing treats to choose from, and they're all on the menu. However, while you contemplate your options, an unease develops in your abdominal region. As you calculate the amount of sugar and carbohydrates and consider how it can affect your blood sugar levels, your thoughts race. Every time they indulge in even the simplest of pleasures, diabetics encounter a difficult mental labyrinth.

This is not an unusual occurrence, since millions of individuals often manage the intricate dance of diabetes. It's a journey that requires constant vigilance, careful label reading, and an endless quest for tasty diabetic recipes. "What can I eat?" is one of many queries that will arise throughout your journey. In what ways can I satisfy both my hunger and my health concerns at the same time? Can I eat what I want without endangering my health?

Our "Diabetic Cookbook" was specifically designed with you in mind. If you find yourself silently acknowledging or nodding along with the issues, then you have arrived to the correct spot. This is more than just a cookbook; it's a travel companion that will help you rediscover the joy of eating without sacrificing your health.

Acknowledging the difficulties posed by a diabetes diagnosis is the initial stride towards conquering the disease. The fear of the unknown, the stress of having to stick to a tight diet, and the worry that comes with grocery shopping are all emotions that are too familiar to us. For people dealing with the difficulties caused by diabetes, it is more than simply a cookbook; it is a lifesaver.

Just what are the benefits of using some of your precious time to perusing these pages? for the reason that this site contains stuff other than recipes. You'll be transported to a galaxy where tasty, low-sugar meals live side by side. Never again will you have to settle for bland food; instead, you'll go on a culinary adventure that celebrates the rich tapestry of tastes from throughout the globe.

The more flexibility it offers its customers is just as brilliant as the meticulously selected selection of tasty recipes in this cookbook. Imagine yourself walking into any kitchen with full self-confidence, knowing that you have all the skills needed to create foods that satisfy the taste buds and feed the body. Now that you're in charge of a culinary symphony tailored to your dietary needs, you won't feel like an outsider in the food industry.

There is a wealth of information in the book that is applicable outside of the kitchen that you will discover as you read on. From reading nutrition labels to handling social situations with grace, this book covers it everything for people living with diabetes. Maintaining a healthy blood sugar level is only the first step in reclaiming your life and enjoying it to the utmost.

I know you're probably asking how I can possibly be the one to show you the way. Neither the time nor the place is right for me to brag about you or my achievements. I am just another traveler on this journey; I have had similar ups and downs, dealt with similar worries, and come out on the other side with a deep understanding of how to enjoy life with diabetes.

Communicating, not instructing, is my intention in penning these pages. In this piece, I will draw on my own experiences, the insights of professionals I've spoken with, and the wisdom of a community that has gone through this before to impart the wisdom I've received. Going on this journey together will have a profound impact on our lives and show us how to turn diabetes into a driving force for living life to the fullest, rather than a limitation.

You are not alone in feeling the disappointment of meals that did not fulfill your requirements or in the weight that dietary limitations put on you, my dear reader. An impassioned plea for a culinary revolution, this cookbook is sure to leave you exclaiming, "This is the book for me!" Here, food serves as both a means of subsistence and an occasion for joy, and I couldn't be happier to have you join us. Along with the "Diabetic Cookbook," you will discover a newfound appreciation for every single meal.

## Comprehending Diabetes

Worldwide, millions of individuals live with the long-term effects of diabetes. The main cause of this condition is a complex interplay between a person's metabolism and their way of life, which together greatly diminish their standard of living. Diabetes is a complicated disease with several subcategories, which this article delves into. It also discusses the condition's origins, risk factors, subtle symptoms, diagnostic tools, and, most significantly, the critical need of proper treatment.

## Diabetes Types

Diabetes is not a singular disease but rather a spectrum of related but distinct health problems. Diabetes encompasses a wide range of health issues rather than just one disease. Diabetes comes in several forms; the most common ones are types 1 and 2, but gestational diabetes and others are less prevalent.

Adolescents and young adults are particularly vulnerable to the autoimmune illness known as type 1 diabetes. An immune system assault and subsequent death of insulin-producing beta cells in the pancreas characterizes this kind of diabetes, which leads to hyperglycemia. To keep their blood sugar levels normal, people with type 1 diabetes must inject themselves with exogenous insulin.

Obesity type 2: Adults often receive a diagnosis of this more prevalent form of the disease. When insulin is not used properly, it leads to this condition. To begin countering this resistance, the pancreas first generates an excess of insulin. Unfortunately, normal blood glucose levels are finally out of the pancreas' control. Some of the lifestyle variables that greatly impact the development of type 2 diabetes include poor nutrition, lack of physical exercise, and behavior, in addition to heredity.

Diabetes In rare cases, a disease known as gestational diabetes can develop during a woman's pregnancy. It's a temporary condition that shows up while you're pregnant. Despite its disappearance after delivery, having it increases the chance of developing type 2 diabetes in later life.

## Reasons and Danger Elements

Both hereditary factors and environmental factors contribute to the development of diabetes. The combination of these two types of risk factors leads to diabetes. A thorough understanding of the problem's causes is essential for developing effective preventative measures.

Having a close relative with diabetes greatly increases a person's risk of getting the condition. If a person has a close family with diabetes, they are more likely to have the disease themselves. An increased chance of developing diabetes is associated with some genetic markers as well.

Features of the environment: The way a person lives their life significantly raises their chances of getting diabetes. The risk of developing type 2 diabetes is increased by leading an inactive lifestyle and eating a diet high in processed sugars and harmful fats. Furthermore, it has been proposed that some chemicals and other environmental variables may contribute to the development of diabetes.

Some believe that being overweight is a major contributor to the development of type 2 diabetes. Because insulin resistance is related with excess adipose tissue, especially in the abdominal area, it is necessary to maintain a healthy weight in order to avoid and manage diabetes.

## Symptoms and Diagnosis

It is critical to diagnose diabetes symptoms in order to start treatment as soon as possible. Some of the most common signs of diabetes are increased thirst, increased frequency of urination, persistent exhaustion, and unexplained weight loss. The signs and symptoms of type 1 and type 2 diabetes might vary from person to person.

The Signs and Symptoms of T1D Symptoms experienced by people with type 1 diabetes can be noticeable and, at times, unexpected. Rapid weight loss, increased hunger, extreme thirst, and the need to urinate often are all possible symptoms. Common adverse effects include sensitivity and fatigue.

Among the signs of type 2 diabetes are: Some people with type 2 diabetes may experience a slow onset of symptoms. Increased thirst, lethargy, frequent urination, and blurred eyesight are common complaints. The need of regular testing is underscored by the fact that many patients go for long stretches without showing any symptoms.

Diagnostic Methods Diagnosing diabetes requires a physician to do both blood tests and a physical examination. Oral glucose tolerance, hemoglobin A1c, and fasting blood sugar tests provide valuable insights into the temporal dynamics of blood sugar levels. Doctors consider a patient's symptoms, medical history, and any risk factors before making a diagnosis.

## Importance of Managing Diabetes

Serious complications affecting nearly every function in the body can result from poorly managed diabetes. An increased risk of infections, nephritis, neuropathy, and cardiovascular problems are among its many negative health effects. Appropriate diabetes treatment is critical for reducing the impact of these risks and leading a fulfilling life.

Cardiovascular illness is already a major risk factor for diabetes, and the condition makes it much worse. To avoid heart-related disorders, it is necessary to take medication, make lifestyle modifications, and have periodic exams. Increased glucose, hypertension, and cholesterol levels are some of these side effects.

Diabetes and Sleep Disorders: Nerve injury (neuropathy) and kidney damage (chronic hyperglycemia) are possible outcomes of chronic hyperglycemia (also known as nephropathy). To manage and avoid these disorders, it is necessary to closely observe the patient, provide medicine regularly, and make lifestyle modifications.

Prevention of Infections Because their immune systems are already weak, people with diabetes are far more likely to have infections. Following vaccination schedules, giving them proper wound care, and checking on them often will help prevent infections.

Enhancing Quality of Life: Optimal management of diabetes extends beyond the alleviation of specific symptoms to encompass overall well-being. People with diabetes may live fulfilling lives if they prioritize a healthy lifestyle, follow their doctor's advice, and schedule periodic appointments.

To effectively manage diabetes, one must grasp its intricacies. By learning about the many kinds of diabetes, where it comes from, what causes it, how to recognize the signs, and how important it is to get a diagnosis early on, people can take charge of their health and work toward a future without diabetes. A life full of resilience, vitality, and wellness may be achieved with effective management of diabetes, which is more than just a medical necessity.

# Basics of Nutrition for People with Diabetes

An individual's dietary habits have a significant impact on their blood sugar levels and general health and wellness, making them an important dance partner in the complex dance of diabetes management. In this chapter, we will look at the fundamental dietary concepts that are important for people with diabetes to follow. The intricate interplay of carbs, proteins, and lipids is one of the topics covered. The importance of controlling portions and eating at the right times, deciphering the glycemic index and glycemic load, and helping readers decipher food label jargon are among subjects covered.

## Carbs, Proteins, and Fats

In discussions about diabetic diet, the function of carbs is front and center. The bulk of the diet consists of carbohydrates. Despite the outmoded notion that carbs should be shunned at all costs, it's critical to understand that there are many types of carbohydrates. Dietary sources of complex carbohydrates include vegetables, legumes, and whole grains. A balanced diet cannot be complete without them. The steady release of glucose helps avoid spikes in blood sugar levels. Due to their quick effect on blood sugar levels, simple carbohydrates—found in abundance in processed meals and refined grains—should be consumed sparingly.

Proteins: It is impossible to keep blood glucose levels steady without proteins. Diabetics can benefit greatly from incorporating them into their diet as they do not impact blood glucose levels. Lean protein sources, such as chicken, fish, tofu, and lentils, are the best way to maintain an energy-rich diet without experiencing the negative blood-sugar fluctuations that are common with high-carb meals.

Making a distinction between good and bad fats is the first step in debunking the notion that fat consumption should be strictly limited. You may keep diabetes under control by eating foods like avocados, almonds, and olive oil, which are rich in monounsaturated and polyunsaturated fats. By improving heart health and keeping you full for longer, these fats help you regulate your weight. Processed and fried meals are common sources of trans and saturated fats, which are bad for you since they raise the risk of cardiovascular disease and insulin resistance.

## Glycemic Index and Glycemic Load

One useful indicator that consumers may use to assist them traverse the vast array of dietary possibilities is the glycemic index (GI) and glycemic load (GL). If people with diabetes are aware of how various foods affect their blood sugar levels, they may make well-informed choices.

Carbohydrates are ranked numerically on the Glycemic Index (GI) based on their tendency to raise blood glucose levels. Foods with a higher glycemic index (GI) take longer to elevate blood sugar levels than those with a lower GI. Diabetics are encouraged to eat low glycemic index (GI) foods so they may better control their blood sugar levels. Some examples of such foods are legumes, vegetables with little carbohydrate, and whole grains.

How Much Sugar Is In There (GL): When compared to the Glycemic Index (GI), which assesses the effects of each dietary item separately, the GL considers both the kind and amount of carbs consumed. It clarifies the effects of various foods on blood sugar levels in a more comprehensive way. One slice of watermelon, for instance, has very little carbs, hence it has a high GI but a low GL. The high water content of the fruit is to blame for this.

## Portion Control and Meal Timing

Regulating Serving Size The adage "everything in moderation" rings particularly true for diabetics trying to control their condition. In order to lower blood sugar spikes, portion control is key. In order to promote mindful eating, it is recommended to use measuring spoons, switch to more conventional meals, and resist the urge to overeat. Blood sugar levels may respond harmoniously to a diet that strikes a good balance between protein, carbohydrates, and fats.

Because of the importance of meal scheduling in diabetes management, time is of the essence. Establishing a regular eating schedule helps keep blood sugar levels stable and regularizes the body's internal clock. Eating healthy snacks in between larger meals and spreading out your meals throughout the day will help keep your blood sugar levels stable. In addition, the timing of carbohydrate consumption in relation to exercise may affect how the body uses glucose. The need of planning meals around regular activities, such exercise and other hobbies, is emphasized by this.

## Reading Food Labels

For many, deciphering the intricate web of food labels is as challenging as solving a jigsaw puzzle. To make educated dietary choices, though, this skill must be mastered. Important topics to focus on include the following:

The portion size: To prevent inadvertently eating more carbs and other nutrients than necessary, it's important to manage portion sizes. Keep in mind that the serving size on the packaging might not be the precise match for your consumption preferences.

Each and every carb: Fibers and sugars are both included in the carbohydrate category in this section. Pay special attention to the breakdown to determine where the carbs are coming from, and choose whole, unprocessed meals.

Because it aids in blood sugar regulation, dietary fiber is a helpful ally for diabetics. A diet rich in fruits, vegetables, whole grains, and other fiber-rich foods should be consumed in large quantities.

Added sugars and naturally occurring sugars in food are two very different things, and although it's true that some sugars are bad for you, it's also important to know the difference. Better control of blood sugar levels is linked to consuming less added sugar.

You may find out what goes into making an item by looking at its ingredient list, which is shown below. Look for products that have few fillers, aren't overly processed, and have clearly recognizable components.

In addition to being crucial for all people living with diabetes, mastering the fundamentals of a diabetic diet is like assembling a well-rounded set of tools for better health and wellness. Understanding the complex interactions between carbs, proteins, and fats; being familiar with the glycemic index and glycemic load; controlling portion sizes and scheduling meals mindfully; and confidently reading food labels may all help people with diabetes navigate the culinary world. Inviting readers to take charge of their nutrition once again and lay the groundwork for a fuller, more balanced life, this is more than just a how-to guide.

# Creating a Diabetic Plate That Is Balanced

To effectively manage diabetes, it is necessary to have access to certain nutrients as well as the knowledge and skills to prepare balanced, nutrient-dense meals. In this chapter, you will find a thorough strategy for controlling your blood sugar levels and your diet. It delves into the realm of healthy snacking, details the intricacies of making well-rounded meals, and takes a look at the Plate Method as a framework.

## The Plate Method

Diabetics might benefit from the Plate Method, a visual aid for meal planning that facilitates the balanced arrangement of foods on the plate. As a practical guide, it offers a simple way to distribute nutrients and regulate portion size.

How Is It Operated? Envision dividing your meal into three equal parts: one quarter for low-fat meats, half for starchy-free veggies, and the other quarter for carbs. When planning healthy meals that contribute to more consistent blood sugar levels, this visual aid is useful.

Most of the veggies on the plate are carb-free, so they don't contain any carbohydrate. In addition to adding flavor and color to the dish, the variety of textures and hues of these veggies make them a good source of fiber, vitamins, and minerals. Think about peppers, broccoli, and cauliflower, all of which are cruciferous veggies. These veggies are great for diabetics to eat because they don't have much of an effect on blood sugar levels.

Proteins Low in Satin In the next section, we'll talk about low-fat proteins. These are the protein building blocks that make you feel full. The alternatives offer a wide selection of substitutes to satisfy diverse dietary restrictions and tastes, including lentils, turkey, salmon, tofu, and chicken, among many others. Proteins are crucial for preventing blood sugar increases following carbohydrate-heavy meals and for keeping blood sugar levels stable throughout the day.

Carbs: The other part of the plate is devoted to carbohydrates, the energy source that need special consideration. For continuous energy without causing a spike in blood sugar levels, choose for whole grains such as brown rice, quinoa, or whole wheat pasta. The Plate Method promotes a healthier diet by highlighting the importance of complex carbohydrates over simple sugars.

## Creating Balanced Meals

The key to creating healthy meals is learning more about different types of food, how much to eat, and what sequence to take nutrients. Even when we exclude the "Plate Method," this remains valid. Delicious, nutritious, and easy to control your blood sugar levels—that is the goal of this recipe book.

To Include a Wide Range of Food Categories: The hallmark of a "balanced lunch" is the presence of many food categories, which permits the intake of a diverse range of nutrients. Along with complex carbs, lean meats, and starch-free vegetables, be sure to incorporate some tasty fats like avocados or olive oil into your diet. With this, you won't get a bloated feeling for as long. When taken together, these vitamins improve one's health and wellness.

The Sizes of Conscious Portions: It is nevertheless crucial to estimate serving sizes accurately, even when using the visual cues provided by the Plate Method. In comparison to carbs, which are around the size of a tennis ball, protein is roughly the size of a regular deck of playing cards. A customized eating regimen may be developed by adjusting the serving sizes at each meal in line with factors such as age, degree of physical activity, and metabolic rate.

Keeping the Right Macronutrient Balance Maintaining healthy blood sugar levels requires careful meal planning that takes into account a balanced macronutrient ratio. To do this, you must make sure that your protein, carb, and fat intake is balanced. To avoid the health risks associated with an imbalanced diet, it's important to aim for a balanced distribution of nutrients. For instance, to avoid spikes in blood sugar, it's best to consume complex carbohydrates with lean protein, as the two foods work together to delay glucose absorption.

Among the many considerations in managing blood sugar levels, meal timing is crucial. The risk of hypoglycemia and dangerously high blood sugar spikes after meals can be reduced by eating at regular intervals throughout the day. The danger of hypoglycemia increases with the length of time that one fasts. In addition, fueling yourself with a healthy meal before exercise makes it easier for the body to do what it has to do.

## Smart Snacking

Snacks are not only a tasty way to eat, but they may also aid in diabetes control if eaten moderately and mindfully. Feeling full for longer and avoiding dangerous spikes in blood sugar can be achieved by eating a nutrient- and fiber-rich diet. An intelligent snack would be this.

Advice on How to Choose Nutritious Snacks: Choose snacks that will help you get the nutrients you need instead of those that are just calories. A handful of nuts, such as walnuts, hummus-topped hashed veggies, or Greek yogurt topped with berries are nutritious snacks that will keep you full for longer.

Timing Your Snack Appropriately: Timing is as crucial as substance when it comes to deciding whether you nibble or not. By eating a snack in between meals, one may stave off ravenous hunger pangs and control portion sizes during mealtimes. In addition, consuming carbohydrates alongside proteins or healthy fats aids in the maintenance of steady blood sugar levels.

A good connection with food may be achieved by paying attention to the bodily signals that show when you're hungry and eating snacks only when you're actually hungry, not because you're bored or out of habit. In addition to the three square meals each day, all of your snacks should be eaten mindfully. You can be sure that every bite is a calculated choice because of this.

Meal planning for people with diabetes is an art form that calls for imagination, scientific understanding, and a complete understanding of one's own dietary needs. The Plate Method provides a helpful framework for meal planning, and the concepts of balanced eating and strategic snacking provide a sophisticated technique to provide the body with the nourishment it needs. Rather than being a dry how-to, this chapter encourages readers to see each meal as a chance to get healthier, better manage their diabetes, and to eat with confidence.

# Essential Ingredients and Tools for the Kitchen

Effective diabetes therapy is sought for in the kitchen, and it's not only because of food philosophy. In this chapter, we'll take a look at the wide variety of diabetic-friendly kitchen gadgets and supplies available. If you want to make your kitchen a place where you feel empowered to cook, this research is for you. From gathering health-conscious cooking skills and buying essential utensils to stocking the pantry with requirements for diabetes, this inquiry offers as a guide for making the kitchen a sanctuary.

## Diabetic-Friendly Pantry Staples

It is important to thoroughly assess the pantry alternatives while planning a diabetic-friendly kitchen. The goal is to find a balance of flavors and nutritional profiles by combining substances. In order to build nutritious, balanced meals, let's take a look at the staples that diabetics should always have on hand.

Instead of processed grains, try eating healthy grains like quinoa, brown rice, and oats. The lower glycemic index of these grains means that they deliver sustained energy rather than the refined varieties' brief spurts.

Legumes include beans, lentils, and chickpeas, among others. The high protein and fiber content of these foods makes them ideal pantry staples for those with diabetes. They help keep blood sugar levels steady and make you feel full for longer.

Nuts and Seeds: Almonds, chia seeds, walnuts, and flaxseeds are some of the most nutrient-dense nuts and seeds. The pantry is where you can find them. Not only are they delicious, but they're also nutritious because to their high fiber, mineral, and healthy fat content.

Healthy Oils: Two of the healthiest oils for your heart are olive and avocado. An important part of these oils is the heart-healthy monounsaturated fats that have no effect on blood sugar levels.

Some studies have shown that vinegars, especially apple cider vinegar, can aid in diabetes management. Several studies have demonstrated that consuming vinegar with meals may have health advantages, including lowering blood sugar levels and increasing insulin sensitivity. Enhance the flavor of meals without adding too much sugar or salt by using aromatic plant materials. Flavor your food with herbs and spices that won't spike your blood sugar levels. Some examples include cilantro, thyme, and basil. Spices like turmeric and cinnamon also work well.

Natural sugar substitutes such as erythritol, stevia, and monk fruit can be used to sweeten food without raising blood sugar levels. These alternatives provide a touch of sweetness without the metabolizing issues associated with traditional sugars.

## Cooking Techniques for Diabetes

Cooking is more than simply a way to make food; it's a kind of culinary magic that transforms raw materials into nutrient-dense finished goods. Cooking techniques that enhance flavor without compromising nutritional content are crucial for diabetics.

Techniques for Cooking That Add Flavor Without Adding Extra Fat You can bring out more flavor without adding a lot of fat when you grill or roast. These techniques reduce the need for extra oils while imparting a delicious smokiness to your meal. This applies to lean meats, vegetables, and fruits as well.

One way to quickly prepare veggies without sacrificing their natural nutrients and color is to cook them gently, like steaming. This is a great strategy for those who wish to enhance the taste of their food without lowering the nutritional value.

The nutritional content and unique texture of proteins and vegetables may be preserved when cooking them quickly in a moderate amount of oil. Without needlessly adding extra fat, this approach adds depth to foods.

Cooking on a Low Flame For those who are always on the go, the slow cooker is a lifesaver. With it, you can make delicious, nutritious meals with little effort. Also, flavors may blend over time in the oven without adding too many extra sweets or fats.

Team Kitchen: If you wish to speed up the process of making meals, you should embrace the concept of cooking in batches. People with diabetes may make sure they have healthful and convenient food alternatives by making more of the essentials and freezing some of it. This means less processed or perhaps harmful options will be necessary for them.

## Must-Have Kitchen Tools

The gadgets that are available for use in a kitchen frequently dictate how productive it is. Individuals managing their diabetes will find that having the appropriate utensils not only simplifies cooking but also helps prepare healthier meals.

A digital kitchen scale is an essential tool for diabetics as healthy portion control is so important to them. People can better control their carbohydrate intake and maintain healthy blood sugar levels by using a digital kitchen scale, which guarantees accurate measures.

The Best Knives in Quality: Having a good, sharp knife set makes meal preparation simpler and faster. Since a clean knife set may be used for everything from slicing vegetables to portioning out meats, it is a necessity when cooking.

Cookware That Dispenses Food Without Using Oil Making meals with a focus on health is encouraged when using cookware that releases food without the need for oil. Non-stick cooking utensils are perfect for grilling or sautéing meals with little to no additional oil because they are simple to clean and do not adhere to food.

If you're looking for creative ways to include more vegetables to your diet, a vegetable spiralizer could be the key. Vegetable spiralizing is a fun and inventive way to increase the amount of nutrients in your diet. It turns veggies like zucchini and carrots into strands that resemble noodles, providing a wholesome alternative to traditional pasta.

Blender or food processor: Blenders and food processors are some of the most useful kitchen appliances since they can be used to make smoothies, purees, and sauces. They are especially helpful for those who want to include a variety of flavors and textures in their diet.

Instant-Read Thermometer: It's critical to accurately determine the ideal cooking temperature, especially when preparing proteins. Meats can be cooked to the perfect temperature without the risk of being overdone or underdone by using an instant-read thermometer.

Slow Cooker: For those who need to manage their diabetes but are pressed for time, using a slow cooker can be beneficial. It lets you cook substantial, high-nutrient meals with a minimal amount of effort on your part.

Getting the right tools and cooking skills, along with stocking the pantry with healthful foods that fit the person's desired level of wellness, are all important steps in transforming a kitchen into a safe haven for diabetics. This chapter is not just a guide; rather, it's an invitation to go on a culinary adventure where every tool and ingredient is a paintbrush, helping to create a painting of delectable and nutritious dishes. People with diabetes can take control of their diabetes treatment by learning a vibrant and sustainable method of food preparation that is both healthful and aesthetically pleasing. All they need are the proper cooking techniques, kitchen tools, and staples for their pantry.

# Additives and Alternatives

A comprehensive knowledge of the many sugar substitutes and sweeteners available is necessary to craft a diabetic-friendly cooking experience. This chapter gives readers a better grasp of sweeteners by delving into natural sugar replacements, discussing artificial sweeteners, and providing diabetic-specific baking guidance.

## Healthy Alternatives to Sugar

Putting your health on the line to become sweet isn't always necessary. Satisfying a sweet appetite and improving overall health are both made possible by enjoying naturally occurring, high-nutrient sugar replacements.

The Stevia rebaudiana plant's leaves are processed into the natural sweetener known as Stevia. Despite its sweetening properties, stevia is lower in carbs and calories than competing sweeteners. Due to its intense sweetness, stevia has become a popular sugar alternative for individuals watching their calorie consumption.

Sake with Monk Fruit: It is well-known that this sugar substitute is both calorie-free and naturally occurring. What this is made of is actually monk fruit. Monk fruit sweetener is appealing to diabetics attempting to regulate their blood sugar levels since it imparts sweetness without causing the same metabolic impact as sugar.

One sugar alcohol that enhances sweetness without affecting blood sugar absorption is erythritol. Both in its processed commercial form and its natural, unprocessed state, which is present in specific fruits. Because it has a negligible effect on the glycemic response, erythritol is a popular sugar alternative in many recipes.

Xylitol is a distinct sugar alcohol that may be made from either maize or birch wood. It has a sweet flavor, but it's lower in calorie density and less of an impact on blood sugar levels than sugar. Xylitol is a sugar replacement that is widely used in baking and cooking.

Sugar derived from coconuts: Coconut sugar has a lower glycemic index than regular white sugar, making it a healthier option, yet it is still classified as a sugar. It is a somewhat healthier option to think about because it contains antioxidants and small quantities of minerals such as zinc and iron.

# Artificial Sweeteners

Despite their reputation, artificial sweeteners do have a function; they are one of the many sugar substitutes that are available. To avoid the calorie and glycemic load of sugar, people often turn to strong sweeteners like these.

An artificial sweetener with less calories than sucrose and around 200 times as much sweetness is aspartame. It is most often seen in diet and sugar-free soft drinks. Since it becomes a mush when exposed to high temperatures, it is best reserved for usage as a tabletop sweetener or in cold beverages.

For a long time, saccharin was one of the most popular artificial sweeteners available. It has a sweetness that is 300–400 times higher than sugar and has no calories. Saccharin is a versatile food ingredient that may be used in baking and other culinary applications due to its inertness when heated.

One artificial sweetener that surpasses sugar in sweetness by a factor of 600 is sucralose. The sugar sucrose is the source from which sucrose is generated. You may use it in the oven and other high-temperature cooking applications since it does not break down. Many sugar-free items contain sucralose, an alternative sweetener.

Tocopherol and other stevia glycosides Rebaudioside A: While stevia does a good job of naturally sweetening food, it is possible to process certain steviol glycosides to make sweeteners that are quite addictive. As an example, here is Rebaudioside A. For example, rebaudioside A is a common sugar replacement that is used in many different foods.

# Baking Tips for Diabetics

People attempting to control their diabetes have unique challenges when baking due to the specific measurements and chemistry involved. The joys of baking don't have to come at the expense of one's attempts to live a healthy lifestyle provided one has the right knowledge and abilities.

Using Flour and Whole Grains Coconut flour, almond flour, or whole wheat flour are some whole-grain alternatives to refined flours that you might want to try. The increased fiber content of these options makes glucose absorption slower.

All-Natural Splendor: Erythritol, stevia, or monk fruit sweetener are all natural alternatives to sugar that you may use in your baked goods. Because some substances may sometimes be sweeter than sugar, it is necessary to reduce the amount used of these sweeteners, thus it is vital to be aware of their sweetness intensity.

Minimize the Use of Added Fats: Moderation is vital when it comes to adding fats to baked products, even if they're essential for taste and texture. To make your meals healthier, try using avocado or olive oil instead of total fat and reducing the amount of extra fat you use.

Boost the Nutrient Density: Baked foods can have their nutritious density increased by adding nuts and seeds. They offer healthy fats and essential nutrients to the dish while also enhancing its flavor and texture.

You may enjoy baked goods in moderation as long as you control your portion sizes. In order to cut back on carbs and calories, it's important to think about serving sizes. Preparing baked items in advance and substituting natural fruit purees for part of the sugar and fat will help you control your portion sizes and avoid overindulging. One option is to use natural fruit purees in place of some of the sugar and fat in the recipes. Without adding extra sugar or fat, you may increase the sweetness and moisture content of a meal by pureeing some pumpkin, mashed bananas, or apple sauce.

Researching alternatives and other sweeteners is a crucial first step in creating a diabetic-friendly kitchen. Diabetics can satisfy their sweet desire with a variety of alternatives, including artificial sweeteners and natural sweeteners like stevia and monk fruit sweetener. With the right techniques and substitutes, baking—often seen as a culinary hurdle for those with diabetes—can become an enjoyable hobby. If you're looking for a resource or just want to learn more about the wonderful world of sugar replacements and sweeteners, this chapter is for you. By following these steps, readers may create a culinary adventure that meets their health objectives while enhancing their passion for food.

# Breakfast Recipes

## 1.    Quinoa and Vegetable Breakfast Dish

- Time Required : 10 mins
- Curing time: 15 mins
- Serves: 2

Ingredients:

- 185g quinoa, rinsed
- 500ml vegetable broth
- 15ml olive oil
- 1 onion, hashed
- 2 bell peppers, hashed
- 1 zucchini, hashed
- 5g smoked paprika
- Salt and pepper to taste
- Fresh herbs

Directions:

1. Bring the vegetable broth to a boil in a saucepan. Simmer, covered, for 15 mins after adding cooked quinoa.
2. In a separate pan, heat the olive oil. Sauté until the onion halves become transparent, then add them.
3. Sauté the bell peppers and zucchini when the veggies have softened.
4. Season with salt and pepper, then stir in the cooked quinoa and smoked paprika. Reduce heat and simmer for two or three more mins.
5. Garnish the quinoa and veggie mix with some chopped fresh herbs before serving.

Nutrition Information: Kcals: 350, Protein: 10g, Fat: 8g, Carbs: 60g, Sugar: 5g, Fiber: 8g, Sodium: 800mg

## 2.    Avocado and Egg Breakfast Wrap

- Time Required : 8 mins
- Curing time: 5 mins
- Serves: 1

Ingredients:

- 1 whole-grain wrap
- 1 ripe avocado, hashed
- 2 eggs
- Salt and pepper to taste
- Fresh herbs

Directions:

1. To cook in a nonstick pan, heat a pan over medium heat.
2. Warm the wrapper by placing it in the pan.
3. The eggs can be scrambled, fried, or poached to your liking in a separate pan.
4. Before topping the heated wrap with fried eggs, fresh herbs, salt, and pepper, spread the hashed avocado on top.
5. Quickly after folding, serve the wrap.

Nutrition Information: Kcals: 420, Protein: 20g, Fat: 28g, Carbs: 30g, Sugar: 1g, Fiber: 12g, Sodium: 400mg

## 3.    Greek Yogurt and Berry Smoothie

- Time Required : 5 mins
- Curing time: 0 mins
- Serves: 2

Ingredients:

- 240g Greek yogurt
- 150g mixed berries strawberries, blueberries, raspberries
- 1 banana

- 15ml honey
- 240ml almond milk
- Ice cubes optional

Directions:

1. Blend together the almond milk, banana, Greek yogurt, mixed berries, and honey.
2. Proceed until there are no more bumps. If desired, garnish with ice cubes.
3. Transfer to glasses and top with ice. Serve right away.

Nutrition Information:

Kcals: 250, Protein: 15g, Fat: 5g, Carbs: 40g, Sugar: 25g, Fiber: 6g, Sodium: 100mg

## 4.    Berry and Yogurt Parfait

- Time Required : 7 mins
- Curing time: 0 mins
- Serves: 2

Ingredients:

- 240g Greek yogurt
- 150g mixed berries
- 40g granola
- 15ml honey
- Fresh mint

Directions:

1. Put the Greek yogurt, granola, and mixed berries in individual glasses.
2. As a finishing touch, sprinkle some fresh mint leaves and drizzle with honey.
3. Take another look at the layers.
4. Come right now.

Nutrition Information: Kcals: 320, Protein: 15g, Fat: 8g, Carbs: 45g, Sugar: 20g, Fiber: 7g, Sodium: 80mg

## 5.    Roasted Vegetable Frittata

- Time Required : 15 mins
- Curing time: 25 mins
- Serves: 4

Ingredients:

- 6 eggs
- 120ml milk
- 150g cherry tomatoes, halved
- 150g zucchini, hashed
- 150g bell peppers, hashed
- 150g spinach
- 60g feta cheese, crumbled
- Salt and pepper to taste

Directions:

1. To begin, bring the oven temperature up to 180 degrees Celsius.
2. Combine the milk and eggs in a basin. To taste, sprinkle with pepper and salt.
3. Toss the zucchini, cherry tomatoes, and bell peppers into an ovenproof pan and cook, stirring occasionally, until cooked through.
4. Toss in the spinach and let it wilt in the pan.
5. After adding the veggies to the pan, pour the egg mixture and top with feta cheese. Bake for 10 mins.
6. The frittata should firm up and begin to turn brown after 20 to 25 mins in the oven.
7. Make equal amounts and distribute.

Nutrition Information: Kcals: 220, Protein: 15g, Fat: 15g, Carbs: 10g, Sugar: 5g, Fiber: 3g, Sodium: 300mg

## 6.    Greek Yogurt and Berry Popsicles

- Time Required : 10 mins
- Freeze Time: 4 hours
- Serves: 6

Ingredients:

- 480g Greek yogurt
- 150g mixed berries strawberries, blueberries, raspberries
- 30ml honey

Directions:

1. Toss the honey and Greek yogurt together in a basin and mix until smooth.
2. Mix in the berries one by one.
3. Fill up the popsicle molds with the mixture using a spoon.
4. Once the four hours have passed, insert the popsicle sticks and refrigerate until they are set.
5. When ready to serve, run the molds under warm water to loosen the popsicles.

Nutrition Information: Kcals: 120, Protein: 8g, Fat: 3g, Carbs: 15g, Sugar: 12g, Fiber: 2g, Sodium: 40mg

## 7. Sweet Potato and Kale Hash

- Time Required : 12 mins
- Curing time: 20 mins
- Serves: 3

Ingredients:

- 2 sweet potatoes, peeled and hashed
- 15ml olive oil
- 1 onion, hashed
- 60g kale, hashed
- 5g smoked paprika
- Salt and pepper to taste
- Poached eggs for serving optional

Directions:

1. Bring hashed sweet potatoes to a boil and cook until soft. After it has emptied, take it out.

2.  Olive oil should be heated in a skillet. The chopped onion should be sautéed until it turns transparent.
3.  Throw in the sweet potatoes and greens that have been hashed and brought to a boil.
4.  Season with salt, pepper, and smoked paprika. Sauté the kale once it has wilted.
5.  You may eat it alone or top it with poached eggs.

Nutrition Information: Kcals: 180, Protein: 4g, Fat: 5g, Carbs: 30g, Sugar: 8g, Fiber: 5g, Sodium: 150mg

## 8.    Tomato and Basil Zoodle Salad

- Time Required : 10 mins
- Curing time: 0 mins
- Serves: 2

Ingredients:

- 2 zucchinis, spiralized into zoodles
- 150g cherry tomatoes, halved
- 60ml balsamic vinegar
- 30ml olive oil
- Fresh basil leaves
- Salt and pepper to taste
- Feta cheese  optional

Directions:

1.  Toss the cherry tomatoes and zoodles in a basin.
2.  Combine the balsamic vinegar and olive oil in a another basin and whisk to combine.
3.  After mixing the zoodles, pour the dressing on top. Coat thoroughly by tossing.
4.  Add the shredded basil leaves to the salad. To taste, sprinkle with pepper and salt.
5.  Serve with feta cheese as a garnish if preferred.

Nutrition Information: Kcals: 160, Protein: 4g, Fat: 12g, Carbs: 12g, Sugar: 8g, Fiber: 3g, Sodium: 100mg

## 9.    Berry Chia Seed Pudding

- Time Required : 5 mins
- Chill Time: 4 hours
- Serves: 2

Ingredients:

- 90g chia seeds
- 360ml almond milk
- 15ml honey
- 5ml vanilla extract
- 150g mixed berries

Directions:

1. Gather the chia seeds, honey, almond milk, and vanilla essence into a basin and combine.
2. After giving it a good stir, cover and put it in the fridge to soak into the chia seeds for at least four hours, or all night.
3. Prior to serving, thoroughly mix the pudding.
4. Before serving, top with a layer of mixed berries.

Nutrition Information: Kcals: 220, Protein: 6g, Fat: 12g, Carbs: 25g, Sugar: 10g, Fiber: 12g, Sodium: 80mg

## 10.    Dark Chocolate and Berry Smoothie Dish

- Time Required : 7 mins
- Curing time: 0 mins
- Serves: 1

Ingredients:

- 240ml almond milk
- 150g mixed berries strawberries, blueberries, raspberries

- 1 banana
- 15g dark cocoa powder
- 15g chia seeds
- Toppings: hashed strawberries, dark chocolate chunks, and granola

Directions:

1. The almond milk, banana, chia seeds, mixed berries, and dark chocolate powder should all be blended together in a blender.
2. Proceed until there are no more bumps. If you want it thinner or thicker, just add more almond milk.
3. Divide the smoothie among serving plates.
4. Top with some granola, bits of dark chocolate, and crushed strawberries.
5. Enjoy a spoonful of grazing and dig in!

Nutrition Information: Kcals: 380, Protein: 8g, Fat: 15g, Carbs: 60g, Sugar: 25g, Fiber: 12g, Sodium: 120mg

## 11.    Quinoa and Vegetable Breakfast Dish

- Time Required : 15 mins
- Curing time: 15 mins
- Serves: 2

Ingredients:

- 185g quinoa, cooked
- 15ml olive oil
- 1 bell pepper, hashed
- 1 zucchini, hashed
- 150g cherry tomatoes, halved
- 2 eggs, poached
- Salt and pepper to taste
- Fresh parsley

Directions:

1. Warm up a little olive oil in a skillet over medium heat.

2. Toss in the shredded zucchini and bell peppers. After the vegetables have come to a boil, simmer them until they are tender.
3. Add the cooked quinoa and cherry tomatoes and mix well. Cook, covered, for another 2-3 mins over low heat.
4. In individual serving dishes, spoon the quinoa and vegetable mixture.
5. Top each platter with a poached egg.
6. Add salt and pepper according to your preference.
7. Garnish each serving with a little fresh parsley.

Nutrition Information: Kcals: 320, Protein: 15g, Fat: 15g, Carbs: 35g, Sugar: 5g, Fiber: 7g, Sodium: 150mg

## 12.    Avocado and Egg Breakfast Wrap

- Time Required : 10 mins
- Curing time: 5 mins
- Serves: 2

Ingredients:

- 2 whole-grain wraps
- 1 avocado, hashed
- 4 eggs, scrambled
- 75g cherry tomatoes, hashed
- 30ml salsa
- Salt and pepper to taste

Directions:

1. The whole-grain tortillas may be heated in a microwave or a dry skillet.
2. Evenly distribute the scrambled eggs, hashed cherry tomatoes, and hashed avocado among the tortillas.
3. Spread salsa on top.
4. To taste, sprinkle with pepper and salt.
5. Before serving, fold the wraps.

Nutrition Information: Kcals: 350, Protein: 15g, Fat: 20g, Carbs: 30g, Sugar: 5g, Fiber: 8g,

Sodium: 300mg

## 13.   Roasted Vegetable Frittata

- Time Required : 15 mins
- Curing time: 25 mins
- Serves: 4

Ingredients:

- 8 huge eggs
- 120ml milk
- 150g cherry tomatoes, halved
- 1 zucchini, hashed
- 1 bell pepper, hashed
- 120g spinach, hashed
- 50g feta cheese, crumbled
- Salt and pepper to taste
- Fresh herbs

Directions:

1. Adjust the oven temperature to 180°C.
2. Combine the milk and eggs in a basin and whisk to combine.
3. Cherry tomatoes, zucchini, bell pepper, and spinach may be sautéed in an ovenproof pan until they are soft.
4. Toss the veggies in the pan with the egg mixture.
5. Top with crumbled feta cheese.
6. Season with pepper and salt.
7. After 20 to 25 mins in the oven, the frittata should be set.
8. Add fresh herbs as a garnish just before serving.

Nutrition Information: Kcals: 280, Protein: 18g, Fat: 18g, Carbs: 12g, Sugar: 5g, Fiber: 3g, Sodium: 350mg

# Lunch Recipes

## 14.  Grilled Chicken Salad with Lemon Vinaigrette

- Time Required : 15 mins
- Curing time: 15 mins
- Serves: 2

Ingredients:

- 300g chicken breast, grilled and hashed
- 180g mixed salad greens
- 150g cherry tomatoes, halved
- 1 cucumber, hashed
- 60ml feta cheese, crumbled
- 60ml black olives, hashed
- Lemon Vinaigrette: 45ml olive oil, 15ml lemon juice, salt, and pepper to taste

Directions:

1. Sprinkle olives, feta cheese, cucumber, cherry tomatoes, and salad leaves onto a large platter.
2. Add a chicken breast that has been grilled and hashed on top.
3. For the vinaigrette, just combine the olive oil, lemon juice, salt, and pepper in a standard mixing basin.
4. Gently pour the vinaigrette over the salad and mix till combined.

5. Serve right away.

Nutrition Information: Kcals: 450, Protein: 35g, Fat: 25g, Carbs: 20g, Sugar: 8g, Fiber: 6g, Sodium: 600mg

## 15. Zucchini Noodles with Pesto and Cherry Tomatoes

- Time Required : 10 mins
- Curing time: 5 mins
- Serves: 2

Ingredients:

- 2 huge zucchinis, spiralized into noodles
- 150g cherry tomatoes, halved
- 60g pesto sauce
- 30g pine nuts, toasted
- Fresh basil leaves

Directions:

1. While the noodles are cooking, sauté the zucchini until they begin to soften.
2. Toss in the cherry tomatoes and cook until done.
3. Add the pesto sauce and stir until combined.
4. After transferring to plates, garnish with toasted pine nuts and fresh basil.
5. Serve right away.

Nutrition Information: Kcals: 320, Protein: 8g, Fat: 25g, Carbs: 18g, Sugar: 8g, Fiber: 5g, Sodium: 300mg

## 16. Lentil and Vegetable Soup

- Time Required : 15 mins
- Curing time: 30 mins
- Serves: 4

Ingredients:

- 200g dried green lentils, rinsed
- 1 onion, hashed
- 2 carrots, hashed
- 2 celery stalks, hashed
- 3 cloves garlic, hashed
- 1 can 400g hashed tomatoes
- 1.5 liters vegetable broth
- 5g cumin
- 5g smoked paprika
- Salt and pepper to taste
- Fresh parsley

Directions:

1. The veggies should be sautéed until they are soft in a big saucepan with the garlic, onions, carrots, and celery.
2. Stir in the lentils, vegetable broth, smoked paprika, cumin, and hashed tomatoes. Season with salt and pepper.
3. Raise the heat to a boil after the lentils are soft, then lower the heat and simmer for 20–30 mins.
4. Season according to your preference.
5. Serve with a sprinkle of finely chopped parsley as a garnish.

Nutrition Information: Kcals: 280, Protein: 15g, Fat: 1g, Carbs: 50g, Sugar: 8g, Fiber: 18g, Sodium: 900mg

## 17.  Cauliflower Crust Pizza with Vegetables

- Time Required : 20 mins
- Curing time: 25 mins
- Serves: 2

Ingredients:

- 1 medium cauliflower, riced
- 1 egg
- 60g mozzarella cheese, shredded

- 30g Parmesan cheese, grated
- 2g dried oregano
- 2g garlic powder
- Salt and pepper to taste
- 120ml tomato sauce
- 150g mixed vegetables bell peppers, cherry tomatoes, spinach
- 30g feta cheese, crumbled
- Fresh basil

Directions:

1. The oven should be adjusted at 200°C.
2. Combine the crushed cauliflower, egg, mozzarella, Parmesan, oregano, garlic powder, salt, and pepper on a platter.
3. Form a crust by pressing the mixture into a flat pan lined with parchment paper.
4. Cook in the oven for fifteen to twenty mins, or until the crust is browned and set.
5. Arrange feta cheese and a variety of vegetables on top of the tomato sauce-covered crust.
6. Ten to fifteen more mins in the oven should do the trick.
7. Before serving, garnish with some fresh basil.

Nutrition Information: Kcals: 320, Protein: 20g, Fat: 18g, Carbs: 25g, Sugar: 8g, Fiber: 8g, Sodium: 800mg

## 18.    Turkey and Quinoa Stuffed Peppers

- Time Required : 20 mins
- Curing time: 30 mins
- Serves: 4

Ingredients:

- 4 huge bell peppers, halved and seeds removed
- 185g quinoa, cooked
- 500g ground turkey
- 1 onion, hashed
- 2 cloves garlic, hashed

- 1 can 400g black beans, drained and rinsed
- 150g corn kernels
- 5g cumin
- 5g chili powder
- Salt and pepper to taste
- 240ml tomato sauce
- 120g cheddar cheese, shredded
- Fresh cilantro

Directions:

1. Preheat oven to 180 degrees Celsius.
2. Sauté the onion and garlic with the ground turkey in a skillet until the turkey is fully cooked.
3. Stir in the corn, black beans, cooked quinoa, cumin, chili powder, salt, and pepper.
4. Spoon the filling into the pepper halves.
5. After stuffing the peppers, cover with tomato sauce and cheddar cheese.
6. Cook in the oven for about 20 to 30 mins, or until the cheese begins to bubble and melt.
7. Toss in with chopped cilantro just before serving.

Nutrition Information: Kcals: 420, Protein: 35g, Fat: 15g, Carbs: 40g, Sugar: 8g, Fiber: 10g, Sodium: 600mg

## 19.   Chickpea and Spinach Curry

- Time Required : 10 mins
- Curing time: 25 mins
- Serves: 4

Ingredients:

- 30ml olive oil
- 1 onion, finely hashed
- 3 cloves garlic, hashed
- 15g ginger, grated
- 20g curry powder

- 1 can 400g chickpeas, drained and rinsed
- 1 can 400ml coconut milk
- 30g baby spinach
- Salt and pepper to taste
- Fresh cilantro

Directions:

1. In a large frying pan, heat the olive oil. Fry the ginger, garlic, and onion until they release their aromas.
2. After a min or two of stirring, add the curry powder.
3. After adding the chickpeas, whisk in the coconut milk. Bring to a simmer and cook for 15–20 mins.
4. Once the young spinach begins to wilt, stir it in.
5. To taste, sprinkle with pepper and salt. For garnish, sprinkle with fresh cilantro.
6. It goes well with quinoa or brown rice.

Nutrition Information: Kcals: 380, Protein: 10g, Fat: 25g, Carbs: 30g, Sugar: 5g, Fiber: 8g, Sodium: 700mg

## 20.    Shrimp and Asparagus Stir-Fry

- Time Required : 15 mins
- Curing time: 10 mins
- Serves: 2

Ingredients:

- 200g shrimp, peeled and deveined
- 1 bunch asparagus, trimmed and cut into 2-inch pieces
- 30ml soy sauce
- 15ml oyster sauce
- 15ml sesame oil
- 15ml rice vinegar
- 15ml hoisin sauce
- 15ml olive oil
- 2 cloves garlic, hashed

- 5g ginger, grated
- Sesame seeds

Directions:

1. The rice vinegar, oyster sauce, sesame oil, hoisin sauce, and soy sauce should be combined in a dish.
2. A large skillet or wok is ideal for heating the olive oil. Put the ginger and garlic in and mix well.
3. Fry the prawns in a wok until they become pink.
4. Sauté additional asparagus until it reaches a crisp-tender texture.
5. Toss the shrimp and asparagus in the sauce. Coat thoroughly by tossing.
6. Top with sesame seeds before serving.

Nutrition Information: Kcals: 320, Protein: 25g, Fat: 18g, Carbs: 15g, Sugar: 5g, Fiber: 5g, Sodium: 1200mg

## 21. Greek Chicken Souvlaki Skewers

- Time Required : 15 mins
- Curing time: 15 mins
- Serves: 4

Ingredients:

- 500g chicken breast, cut into cubes
- 60ml olive oil
- 30ml lemon juice
- 5g dried oregano
- 2 cloves garlic, hashed
- Salt and pepper to taste
- Cherry tomatoes and red onion for skewering
- Tzatziki sauce for serving

Directions:

1. Toss the garlic, lemon juice, olive oil, dried oregano, salt, and pepper on a dish.
2. For a minimum of fifteen mins, marinate the chicken cubes in the marinade.

3. Chicken, cherry tomatoes, and red onion are stuffed onto skewers.
4. Grill the chicken skewers for 10 to 15 mins each.
5. Garnish with tzatziki sauce before serving.
6. The olive oil, garlic, lemon juice, dried oregano, salt, and pepper should be mixed together on a dish.
7. Marinating the chicken cubes in the marinade for fifteen mins is a must.
8. Red onion, cherry tomatoes, and marinated chicken are threaded onto skewers.
9. Cook the chicken skewers on the grill for 10–15 mins each.
10. Add tzatziki sauce and serve.

Nutrition Information: Kcals: 280, Protein: 25g, Fat: 18g, Carbs: 5g, Sugar: 2g, Fiber: 1g, Sodium: 400mg

## 22.    Cucumber and Tuna Salad

- Time Required : 10 mins
- Curing time: 0 mins
- Serves: 2

Ingredients:

- 2 cucumbers, thinly hashed
- 2 cans 200g each tuna, drained
- 60g red onion, thinly hashed
- 30g Kalamata olives, hashed
- 60ml olive oil
- 30ml red wine vinegar
- 5g dried oregano
- Salt and pepper to taste
- Feta cheese

Directions:

1. Put the tuna, olives, red onion, and cucumbers that have been hashed onto a plate.
2. Mix the olive oil, red wine vinegar, dried oregano, salt, and pepper in a conventional dish.
3. After adding the dressing, gently toss the salad to combine.

4. Garnish with a little feta crumble.

Nutrition Information:

Kcals: 320, Protein: 30g, Fat: 18g, Carbs: 10g, Sugar: 5g, Fiber: 3g, Sodium: 700mg

## 23.   Ratatouille with Quinoa

- Time Required : 20 mins
- Curing time: 30 mins
- Serves: 4

Ingredients:

- 1 eggplant, hashed
- 1 zucchini, hashed
- 1 yellow bell pepper, hashed
- 1 red onion, hashed
- 3 cloves garlic, hashed
- 1 can 400g hashed tomatoes
- 30ml tomato paste
- 5g dried thyme
- 5g dried rosemary
- Salt and pepper to taste
- 185g quinoa, cooked
- Fresh basil

Directions:

1. Steam or sauté the red onion, bell pepper, eggplant, zucchini, and garlic in a large skillet until the vegetables are soft.
2. Include the tomato paste, salt, pepper, dried rosemary and thyme, and the mashed tomatoes. Bring to a simmer and cook for 15–20 mins.
3. Arrange cooked quinoa on top of the ratatouille.
4. Before serving, garnish with some fresh basil.

Nutrition Information: Kcals: 320, Protein: 10g, Fat: 8g, Carbs: 55g, Sugar: 12g, Fiber: 12g, Sodium: 700mg

## 24.   Turkey and Black Bean Chili

- Time Required : 15 mins
- Curing time: 30 mins
- Serves: 6

Ingredients:

- 500g ground turkey
- 1 onion, hashed
- 2 bell peppers, hashed
- 3 cloves garlic, hashed
- 2 cans 400g each black beans, drained and rinsed
- 1 can 400g hashed tomatoes
- 30g chili powder
- 5g cumin
- 5g paprika
- Salt and pepper to taste
- Fresh cilantro

Directions:

1. Make a roux with ground turkey, peppers, onions, and garlic in a large saucepan.
2. After the tomatoes have been mashed, add the black beans, chili powder, cumin, paprika, salt, and pepper. Mix everything together.
3. To make the chili thicker and to let the flavors soak in, simmer it for 20 to 25 mins.
4. Before serving hot, taste and adjust spice. Garnish with chopped cilantro.

Nutrition Information: Kcals: 380, Protein: 25g, Fat: 15g, Carbs: 40g, Sugar: 8g, Fiber: 12g, Sodium: 800mg

## 25.   Caprese Salad Skewers

- Time Required : 10 mins
- Curing time: 0 mins
- Serves: 4

Ingredients:

- 1 pint cherry tomatoes
- 200g mozzarella balls
- Fresh basil leaves
- Balsamic glaze for drizzling

Directions:

1. Thread fresh basil leaves onto skewers and top with cherry tomatoes and mozzarella balls.
2. On a serving platter, arrange the skewers.
3. Serve immediately after drizzling with balsamic glaze.

Nutrition Information: Kcals: 180, Protein: 12g, Fat: 12g, Carbs: 10g, Sugar: 5g, Fiber: 2g, Sodium: 300mg

## 26.  Baked Cod with Mediterranean Salsa

- Time Required : 15 mins
- Curing time: 20 mins
- Serves: 2

Ingredients:

- 2 cod fillets
- 15ml olive oil
- 5g dried oregano
- Salt and pepper to taste

Mediterranean Salsa:

- 150g cherry tomatoes, 1/2 cucumber, 30g red onion, 30ml olive oil, 15ml balsamic vinegar, 15g Kalamata olives, hashed, fresh parsley

Directions:

1. The oven should be adjusted at 200°C.

2. Season the fish fillets on a narrow baking sheet. Toss in with salt, pepper, and dry oregano. Pour olive oil over the top.
3. To make sure the fish is cooked through and flaky, bake it for around 15 to 20 mins.
4. In a basin, mix together the red onion, cucumber, olive oil, balsamic vinegar, and washed cherry tomatoes. Set aside while the cod bakes. Then, create the Mediterranean salsa.
5. Top the cooked fish with a layer of Mediterranean salsa and garnish with fresh parsley.

Nutrition Information: Kcals: 320, Protein: 25g, Fat: 18g, Carbs: 15g, Sugar: 5g, Fiber: 4g, Sodium: 400mg

## 27.   Quinoa and Black Bean Burrito Dish

- Time Required : 15 mins
- Curing time: 15 mins
- Serves: 4

Ingredients:

- 185g quinoa, cooked
- 1 can 400g black beans, drained and rinsed
- 150g corn kernels
- 150g cherry tomatoes, halved
- 1 avocado, hashed
- 60g red onion, finely hashed
- Fresh cilantro
- Lime wedges for serving

Directions:

1. Throw cooked quinoa, black beans, corn kernels, avocado, red onion, and cherry tomatoes onto a dish. Serve.
2. Mix lightly by tossing.
3. Serve with a sprig of fresh cilantro and a slice of lime for garnish.

Nutrition Information: Kcals: 380, Protein: 15g, Fat: 15g, Carbs: 50g, Sugar: 5g, Fiber: 12g,

Sodium: 600mg

## 28. Mediterranean Chickpea Salad

- Time Required : 10 mins
- Curing time: 0 mins
- Serves: 4

Ingredients:

- 2 cans 400g each chickpeas, drained and rinsed
- 1 cucumber, hashed
- 150g cherry tomatoes, halved
- 60g red onion, finely hashed
- 30g Kalamata olives, hashed
- 60ml olive oil
- 30ml red wine vinegar
- 5g dried oregano
- Salt and pepper to taste
- Feta cheese

Directions:

1. Combine the chickpeas, green olives, cherry tomatoes, red onion, and cucumber in a large basin.
2. Mix the olive oil, red wine vinegar, dried oregano, salt, and pepper in a conventional dish.
3. After adding the dressing, gently toss the salad to combine.
4. Before serving, sprinkle crumbled feta cheese over top.

Nutrition Information: Kcals: 320, Protein: 15g, Fat: 18g, Carbs: 30g, Sugar: 5g, Fiber: 8g, Sodium: 800mg

## 29. Tomato and Basil Zoodle Salad

- Time Required : 10 mins
- Curing time: 0 mins

- Serves: 2

Ingredients:

- 2 zucchinis, spiralized into zoodles
- 150g cherry tomatoes, halved
- 60ml balsamic vinegar
- 30ml olive oil
- Fresh basil leaves
- Salt and pepper to taste
- Feta cheese  optional

Directions:

1. Toss the cherry tomatoes and zoodles in a basin.
2. Combine the balsamic vinegar and olive oil in a another basin and whisk to combine.
3. After mixing the zoodles, pour the dressing on top. Coat thoroughly by tossing.
4. Add the shredded basil leaves to the salad. To taste, sprinkle with pepper and salt.
5. Serve with feta cheese as a garnish if preferred.

Nutrition Information: Kcals: 160, Protein: 4g, Fat: 12g, Carbs: 12g, Sugar: 8g, Fiber: 3g, Sodium: 100mg

## 30.   Turkey and Vegetable Skillet

- Time Required : 15 mins
- Curing time: 20 mins
- Serves: 4

Ingredients:

- 500g ground turkey
- 15ml olive oil
- 1 onion, hashed
- 2 bell peppers, hashed
- 2 zucchinis, hashed
- 3 cloves garlic, hashed
- 5g dried Italian herbs
- Salt and pepper to taste
- Fresh parsley

Directions:

1. Brown the ground turkey in a large pan coated with olive oil.
2. Hashed onion, bell pepper, zucchini, garlic, and garlic powder should be added. Get the veggies cooked until they're soft.
3. Toss with some dried Italian herbs, salt, and pepper.
4. Before serving, sprinkle with some fresh parsley.

Nutrition Information: Kcals: 320, Protein: 25g, Fat: 18g, Carbs: 15g, Sugar: 5g, Fiber: 4g, Sodium: 600mg

## 31.   Grilled Shrimp and Vegetable Skewers

- Time Required : 20 mins
- Curing time: 10 mins
- Serves: 2

Ingredients:

- 200g shrimp, peeled and deveined
- 1 zucchini, hashed
- 1 red bell pepper, hashed
- 1 yellow bell pepper, hashed
- 1 red onion, hashed
- 60ml olive oil
- 30ml lemon juice
- 2 cloves garlic, hashed
- 5g dried oregano
- Salt and pepper to taste

Directions:

1. A meal should be prepared by combining olive oil, lemon juice, garlic, dried oregano, salt, and pepper.
2. Skewer the prawns and veggies.
3. Combine the olive oil and brush it onto the skewers.
4. The shrimp should become opaque after 5 mins on either side of the grill.
5. Warm the food again.

Nutrition Information: Kcals: 280, Protein: 20g, Fat: 18g, Carbs: 15g, Sugar: 5g, Fiber: 4g, Sodium: 400mg

## 32.    Eggplant and Red Lentil Curry

- Time Required : 15 mins
- Curing time: 25 mins
- Serves: 4

Ingredients:

- 1 huge eggplant, hashed
- 200g red lentils, rinsed
- 1 onion, hashed
- 3 cloves garlic, hashed

- 15g curry powder
- 5g cumin
- 1 can 400ml coconut milk
- 1 can 400g hashed tomatoes
- Salt and pepper to taste
- Fresh cilantro

Directions:

1. While the eggplant is cooking, add the red lentils, onion, and garlic to a saucepan and sauté until the eggplant is tender.
2. Once fragrant, add the cumin and curry powder.
3. Combine the diced tomatoes with the coconut milk. Simmer for 20–25 mins.
4. To taste, sprinkle with pepper and salt.
5. Toss in with chopped cilantro just before serving.

Nutrition Information: Kcals: 380, Protein: 15g, Fat: 18g, Carbs: 45g, Sugar: 8g, Fiber: 15g, Sodium: 700mg

## 33. Turkey and Cranberry Lettuce Wraps

- Time Required : 15 mins
- Curing time: 10 mins
- Serves: 4

Ingredients:

- 500g ground turkey
- 15ml olive oil
- 1 onion, hashed
- 120ml low-sugar cranberry sauce
- 5g dried sage
- Salt and pepper to taste
- Iceberg lettuce leaves for wrapping

Directions:

1. Saute the ground turkey in olive oil in a skillet.
2. To get the onion soft, cook it for approximately 5 mins.
3. Combine the cranberry sauce, dried sage, salt, and pepper in a basin. Heat in a pan until done.
4. Distribute the turkey mixture among the iceberg lettuce leaves using a spoon.
5. Distribute as wraps.

Nutrition Information: Kcals: 320, Protein: 25g, Fat: 18g, Carbs: 15g, Sugar: 8g, Fiber: 2g, Sodium: 400mg

## 34.    Lentil and Mushroom Stuffed Bell Peppers

- Time Required : 20 mins
- Curing time: 30 mins
- Serves: 4

Ingredients:

- 4 huge bell peppers, halved and seeds removed
- 200g green lentils, cooked
- 200g mushrooms, finely hashed
- 1 onion, hashed
- 2 cloves garlic, hashed
- 5g dried thyme
- 5g dried rosemary
- Salt and pepper to taste
- 1 can 400g hashed tomatoes
- 120ml vegetable broth
- Fresh parsley

Directions:

1. Set the oven temperature to 180°C.
2. In a pan, sauté the garlic, onion, and mushrooms until they are tender.
3. Season with salt and pepper, then stir in the cooked lentils, dried thyme, rosemary, and rosemary.
4. Spoon 1/2 cup of the lentil and mushroom mixture into each bell pepper.

5. The hashed tomatoes and vegetable broth should be combined in a basin. Pour it over the peppers that are packed.
6. Roast peppers for 25 to 30 mins, or until they become soft.
7. Before serving, sprinkle with some fresh parsley.

Nutrition Information: Kcals: 320, Protein: 15g, Fat: 5g, Carbs: 55g, Sugar: 12g, Fiber: 12g, Sodium: 800mg

## 35.  Greek Chicken and Vegetable Skillet

- Time Required : 15 mins
- Curing time: 20 mins
- Serves: 4

Ingredients:

- 500g chicken breast, hashed
- 15ml olive oil
- 1 red bell pepper, hashed
- 1 yellow bell pepper, hashed
- 1 zucchini, hashed
- 150g cherry tomatoes, halved
- 2 cloves garlic, hashed
- 5g dried oregano
- Salt and pepper to taste
- Feta cheese
- Fresh parsley

Directions:

1. In a pan, sauté the hashed chicken in olive oil over medium-high heat until it is cooked through.
2. Toss in the oregano, garlic, zucchini, cherry tomatoes, peppers (both red and yellow), salt, and pepper.
3. Keep cooking on low heat until the vegetables are soft and the chicken is well covered with the spices.
4. For decoration, sprinkle over some crumbled feta cheese and fresh parsley.

Nutrition Information: Kcals: 300, Protein: 30g, Fat: 12g, Carbs: 15g, Sugar: 8g, Fiber: 5g, Sodium: 600mg

## 36. Cabbage and Turkey Sauté

- Time Required : 15 mins
- Curing time: 15 mins
- Serves: 4

Ingredients:

- 500g ground turkey
- 15ml olive oil
- 1 standard cabbage, shredded
- 2 carrots, julienned
- 2 cloves garlic, hashed
- 5g ground cumin
- 5g smoked paprika
- Salt and pepper to taste
- Fresh cilantro

Directions:

1. Cook the ground turkey in a large pan with olive oil until it browns.
2. Toss in the minced garlic, carrots cut into thin strips, cabbage shreds, cumin powder, paprika with a smokey flavor, salt, and pepper.
3. Once the turkey is cooked through, add the cabbage and continue simmering over medium heat, stirring often, for a few more mins.
4. Make any necessary adjustments to the seasoning.
5. Toss in some chopped cilantro right before serving for a garnish.

Nutrition Information: Kcals: 320, Protein: 25g, Fat: 18g, Carbs: 20g, Sugar: 8g, Fiber: 8g, Sodium: 600mg

## 37.    Turkey and Sweet Potato Hash

- Time Required : 20 mins
- Curing time: 20 mins
- Serves: 4

Ingredients:

- 500g ground turkey
- 2 sweet potatoes, hashed
- 1 onion, hashed
- 2 cloves garlic, hashed
- 5g ground cumin
- 5g chili powder
- Salt and pepper to taste
- Fresh parsley
- Fried eggs for serving optional

Directions:

1. In a large skillet, brown the ground turkey until it is well cooked.
2. Incorporate the ground chili powder, cumin, onion, and garlic, along with the hashed sweet potatoes and any other ingredients that you choose.
3. The sweet potatoes will soften and the turkey will absorb the flavor if simmered for long enough.
4. If you'd like, you may serve it with butter-cooked eggs on the side and top it with fresh parsley.

Nutrition Information: Kcals: 350, Protein: 25g, Fat: 15g, Carbs: 35g, Sugar: 8g, Fiber: 6g, Sodium: 600mg

## 38.    Cauliflower and Chickpea Tacos

- Time Required : 20 mins
- Curing time: 15 mins
- Serves: 4

Ingredients:

- 1 head cauliflower, cut into florets
- 1 can 400g chickpeas, drained and rinsed
- 30ml olive oil
- 5g cumin
- 5g smoked paprika
- 2g garlic powder
- Salt and pepper to taste
- 8 standard corn tortillas
- Avocado slices
- Fresh cilantro

Directions:

1. Preheat oven to 200°C.
2. Sprinkle the chickpeas and cauliflower florets with salt, pepper, garlic powder, cumin, and smoked paprika. Toss in the olive oil.
3. To get a golden cauliflower and crispy chickpeas, bake for 15 to 20 mins.
4. Warm up some corn tortillas and stuff them with the roasted chickpea and cauliflower.
5. Slice some avocado and top with some fresh cilantro for a garnish.

Nutrition Information: Kcals: 280, Protein: 10g, Fat: 12g, Carbs: 35g, Sugar: 5g, Fiber: 10g, Sodium: 400mg

# Dinner Recipes

## 39.   Baked Salmon with Dill and Lemon

- Time Required : 10 mins
- Curing time: 15 mins
- Serves: 2

Ingredients:

- 2 salmon fillets
- 30ml olive oil
- 15g fresh dill, hashed
- 1 lemon, hashed
- Salt and pepper to taste

Directions:

1. Preheat oven to 200°C.
2. Lay out the salmon fillets flat on a baking sheet.
3. Before tossing in the fresh dill, add the salt, pepper, and olive oil.
4. Add the lemon wedges.
5. Cook the salmon in the oven for 12–15 mins, or until it flakes easily when tested with a fork.

Nutrition Information: Kcals: 300, Protein: 25g, Fat: 20g, Carbs: 2g, Sugar: 0g, Fiber: 1g, Sodium: 150mg

## 40.   Baked Chicken with Rosemary and Garlic

- Time Required : 10 mins
- Curing time: 25 mins
- Serves: 4

Ingredients:

- 4 boneless, skinless chicken breasts
- 30ml olive oil
- 10g fresh rosemary, hashed
- 4 cloves garlic, hashed
- Salt and pepper to taste

Directions:

1. The oven should be set at 200°C.
2. Before baking the chicken breasts, set them on a baking sheet.
3. For flavor, sprinkle with salt and pepper and season with sliced garlic and fresh rosemary. Drizzle it with olive oil.
4. After 20–25 mins in the oven, the chicken should be cooked through, reaching an internal temperature of 165 degrees.

Nutrition Information: Kcals: 280, Protein: 30g, Fat: 15g, Carbs: 1g, Sugar: 0g, Fiber: 0g, Sodium: 120mg

## 41.  Roasted Brussels Sprouts with Balsamic Glaze

- Time Required : 10 mins
- Curing time: 20 mins
- Serves: 4

Ingredients:

- 500g Brussels sprouts, trimmed and halved
- 30ml olive oil
- 30ml balsamic glaze
- Salt and pepper to taste

Directions:

1. The oven should be set at 200°C.
2. Toss the Brussels sprouts with the olive oil and then add the salt and pepper.
3. Lay them out on a baking sheet in one even layer.
4. The skin should be golden brown and crispy after 20 mins of cooking over high heat.

5. Finish it off with a drizzle of balsamic glaze before serving.

Nutrition Information: Kcals: 120, Protein: 4g, Fat: 7g, Carbs: 14g, Sugar: 4g, Fiber: 5g, Sodium: 30mg

## 42.  Spinach and Goat Cheese Stuffed Chicken Breast

- Time Required : 15 mins
- Curing time: 25 mins
- Serves: 2

Ingredients:

- 2 boneless, skinless chicken breasts
- 30g fresh spinach
- 60g goat cheese
- 15ml olive oil
- Salt and pepper to taste

Directions:

1. The oven should be adjusted at 200°C.
2. Every single chicken breast need to be adorned with a butterfly.
3. To taste, sprinkle with pepper and salt.
4. Sauté the spinach until it starts to wilt.
5. Top each chicken breast with a layer of sautéed spinach and spread goat cheese on the other side.
6. Use toothpicks to tuck the chicken breasts after folding them.
7. In an ovenproof skillet, heat the olive oil and sear the chicken on both sides.
8. Roast the chicken for 20 to 25 mins, or until it's cooked through, after placing the pan in the oven.

Nutrition Information: Kcals: 320, Protein: 35g, Fat: 18g, Carbs: 2g, Sugar: 0g, Fiber: 1g, Sodium: 200mg

## 43.    Mediterranean Quinoa Dish

- Time Required : 15 mins
- Curing time: 15 mins
- Serves: 4

Ingredients:

- 185g quinoa, cooked
- 150g cherry tomatoes, halved
- 1 cucumber, hashed
- 60g Kalamata olives, hashed
- 30g red onion, finely hashed
- 75g feta cheese, crumbled
- 30ml olive oil
- 15ml red wine vinegar
- 5g dried oregano
- Salt and pepper to taste

Directions:

1. Toss the cooked quinoa with the cucumber, red onion, cherry tomatoes, feta cheese, and Kalamata olives in a large shallow basin.
2. Mix the olive oil, red wine vinegar, dried oregano, salt, and pepper in a conventional dish.
3. After adding the dressing, gently stir the quinoa mixture.
4. Allow to reach room temperature.

Nutrition Information: Kcals: 320, Protein: 10g, Fat: 18g, Carbs: 30g, Sugar: 5g, Fiber: 8g, Sodium: 700mg

## 44.    Cauliflower and Broccoli Gratin

- Time Required : 15 mins
- Curing time: 25 mins
- Serves: 4

Ingredients:

- 1 cauliflower, cut into florets
- 1 broccoli, cut into florets
- 30g butter
- 20g flour
- 240ml unsweetened almond milk
- 100g cheddar cheese, shredded
- Salt and pepper to taste
- Fresh parsley

Directions:

1. The oven should be set at 200°C.
2. The best way to get broccoli and cauliflower tender and crisp is to steam them.
3. Melt the butter in a saucepan over medium heat.
4. To make a paste, add the flour and stir well.
5. Blend in the almond milk gradually until completely smooth.
6. After the sauce has thickened, stir in the melted cheddar cheese.
7. To taste, sprinkle with pepper and salt.
8. Toss the broccoli and cauliflower that have been cooked with the cheese sauce and place in a baking tray.
9. For 20 to 25 mins, or until bubbling and lightly browned, bake.
10. Serve with a sprinkle of fresh parsley for garnish.

Nutrition Information: Kcals: 280, Protein: 12g, Fat: 20g, Carbs: 15g, Sugar: 4g, Fiber: 6g, Sodium: 300mg

## 45.    Eggplant and Tomato Gratin

- Time Required : 20 mins
- Curing time: 30 mins
- Serves: 4

Ingredients:

- 2 eggplants, hashed

- 4 tomatoes, hashed
- 30ml olive oil
- 2 cloves garlic, hashed
- 5g dried thyme
- 100g Parmesan cheese, grated
- Salt and pepper to taste
- Fresh basil

Directions:

1. Preheat oven to 200°C.
2. Arrange the eggplant slices and tomato slices in a baking dish in an alternating fashion.
3. Add olive oil, salt, pepper, dried thyme, and crushed garlic. Season to taste.
4. Finish it off with a dusting of grated Parmesan.
5. Cook in the oven for twenty-five to thirty mins, or until the veggies are tender and the top is golden.
6. Garnish with some finely chopped basil right before serving.

Nutrition Information: Kcals: 240, Protein: 8g, Fat: 15g, Carbs: 20g, Sugar: 8g, Fiber: 8g, Sodium: 400mg

## 46.   Salmon and Asparagus Foil Pack

- Time Required : 15 mins
- Curing time: 20 mins
- Serves: 2

Ingredients:

- 2 salmon fillets
- 1 bunch asparagus, trimmed
- 30ml olive oil
- 2 cloves garlic, hashed
- Lemon slices
- Salt and pepper to taste

Directions:

1. Preheat the oven to 200 degrees Celsius.
2. Lay down a sheet of foil and set each salmon fillet on top.
3. Arrange the spears of asparagus in a circular pattern around the fish.
4. Drizzle with olive oil and season with salt, pepper, and crushed garlic.
5. Sprinkle the lemon slices on top.
6. Use three quarters of the aluminum foil to form a package.
7. In a preheated oven, bake the salmon for about 15 to 20 mins, or until opaque throughout.

Nutrition Information: Kcals: 320, Protein: 30g, Fat: 20g, Carbs: 8g, Sugar: 4g, Fiber: 4g, Sodium: 150mg

## 47.   Spaghetti Squash with Tomato and Basil Sauce

- Time Required : 15 mins
- Curing time: 45 mins
- Serves: 4

Ingredients:

- 1 spaghetti squash, halved and seeds removed
- 30ml olive oil
- 2 cloves garlic, hashed
- 4 tomatoes, hashed
- 10g fresh basil, hashed
- Salt and pepper to taste
- Parmesan cheese

Directions:

1. The oven should be set at 200°C.
2. Set a flat pan on a cutting surface and place the spaghetti squash pieces on top.
3. Rub in some pepper, salt, and chopped garlic. Pour olive oil over the top.
4. After about 45 mins in the oven, the squash should be soft enough to penetrate with a fork.

5. Combine the mashed tomatoes, chopped basil, sea salt, and pepper in a saucepan. To get the tomatoes soft, simmer them for a while.
6. Make "noodles" by scraping the spaghetti squash with a fork.
7. Glaze with basil and tomato sauce.
8. Before serving, sprinkle a little Parmesan cheese on top.

Nutrition Information: Kcals: 180, Protein: 3g, Fat: 10g, Carbs: 22g, Sugar: 8g, Fiber: 4g, Sodium: 150mg

## 48.    Shrimp and Zucchini Noodle Stir-Fry

- Time Required : 15 mins
- Curing time: 10 mins
- Serves: 4

Ingredients:

- 500g shrimp, peeled and deveined
- 4 zucchinis, spiralized into noodles
- 30ml soy sauce
- 15ml sesame oil
- 15ml rice vinegar
- 15ml hoisin sauce
- 2 cloves garlic, hashed
- 5g ginger, grated
- Green onions
- Sesame seeds

Directions:

1. Mix together the rice vinegar, hoisin sauce, toasted sesame oil, and soy sauce on a dish.
2. Heat a large skillet or wok over medium-high heat.
3. Grate the ginger and mince the garlic for the shrimp. Shrimp should be stir-fried until pink and cooked through.
4. Toss the zucchini noodles in a pan and sauté for a couple of mins.
5. Add the noodles and shrimp, then drizzle with the sauce. Add enough to coat.

6. Sprinkle toasted sesame seeds and hashed green onions over each plate before serving.

Nutrition Information: Kcals: 280, Protein: 25g, Fat: 10g, Carbs: 20g, Sugar: 10g, Fiber: 5g, Sodium: 800mg

## 49.    Greek Salad with Grilled Chicken

- Time Required : 15 mins
- Curing time: 15 mins
- Serves: 4

Ingredients:

- 500g chicken breast, grilled and hashed
- 1 cucumber, hashed
- 150g cherry tomatoes, halved
- 75g Kalamata olives, hashed
- 100g feta cheese, crumbled
- 30g red onion, thinly hashed
- 30ml olive oil
- 30ml red wine vinegar
- 5g dried oregano
- Salt and pepper to taste

Directions:

1. In a big platter, mix grilled chicken breasts with sliced red onion, cherry tomatoes, crumbled feta cheese, Kalamata olives, cucumber, and thinly sliced red onion.
2. Melt the olive oil, vinegar, dried oregano, salt, and pepper in a regular basin.
3. Toss the salad slightly after dressing has been added.
4. Serve immediately after cooking.

Nutrition Information: Kcals: 320, Protein: 30g, Fat: 18g, Carbs: 15g, Sugar: 5g, Fiber: 3g, Sodium: 600mg

## 50.    Baked Eggplant Parmesan

- Time Required : 20 mins
- Curing time: 30 mins
- Serves: 4

Ingredients:

- 2 huge eggplants, hashed
- 100g breadcrumbs
- 50g Parmesan cheese, grated
- 2 eggs, beaten
- 480ml marinara sauce
- 100g mozzarella cheese, shredded
- Fresh basil

Directions:

1. The oven should be set at 200°C.
2. Breadcrumbs and grated Parmesan should be used to coat the eggplant slices after dipping them in beaten eggs.
3. In a nonstick skillet, add the sliced eggplant that has been greased.
4. Grill for approximately 20 mins, or until crisp and golden.
5. Arrange the roasted eggplant slices in a baking dish with the shredded mozzarella cheese and marinara sauce.
6. Replay all of the levels.
7. Keep baking for another ten mins, or until the cheese begins to bubble and melt.
8. Before serving, garnish with some fresh basil.

Nutrition Information: Kcals: 280, Protein: 15g, Fat: 12g, Carbs: 30g, Sugar: 10g, Fiber: 6g, Sodium: 800mg

## 51.    Shrimp and Quinoa Paella

- Time Required : 15 mins
- Curing time: 25 mins
- Serves: 4

Ingredients:

- 500g shrimp, peeled and deveined
- 185g quinoa, uncooked
- 1 onion, hashed
- 2 bell peppers, hashed 1 red, 1 yellow
- 3 cloves garlic, hashed
- 5g smoked paprika
- 2g saffron threads optional
- 480ml vegetable broth
- 1 can 400g hashed tomatoes
- Salt and pepper to taste
- Fresh parsley

Directions:

1. Rinse the quinoa under cold water.
2. The shrimp should be sautéed until they become pink in a large skillet or paella pan. Detach and place aside.
3. In the same skillet, sauté the onion, bell peppers, and hashed garlic until they are soft.
4. Add the saffron threads and smoked paprika, and stir to combine.
5. Whisk in the quinoa that has been rinsed, the vegetable stock, and the chopped tomatoes. Reduce heat to low and simmer.
6. Once the quinoa is done, cook it covered over low heat for around 15 to 20 mins.
7. After adding the cooked shrimp, fold it in.
8. To taste, sprinkle with pepper and salt.
9. Serve with a sprinkle of fresh parsley for garnish.

Nutrition Information: Kcals: 350, Protein: 25g, Fat: 10g, Carbs: 40g, Sugar: 8g, Fiber: 6g, Sodium: 800mg

- Time Required : 10 mins
- Curing time: 5 mins
- Serves: 2

Ingredients:

- 4 zucchinis, spiralized into noodles
- 30ml olive oil
- 2 cloves garlic, hashed
- 240ml cherry tomatoes, halved
- 10g fresh basil, hashed
- 25g Parmesan cheese, grated
- Salt and pepper to taste

Directions:

1. In a large saucepan set over medium heat, warm the olive oil.
2. Before adding the hashed garlic, sauté the garlic till it releases its scent.
3. Toss up some zucchini noodles and cherry tomatoes for a delicious skillet meal. Reduce heat and simmer for three or five mins once veggies are crisp-tender.
4. Incorporate some Parmesan cheese and freshly chopped basil.
5. Before serving, season with a pinch of salt and pepper.
6. Serve right away when cooking is finished.

Nutrition Information: Kcals: 180, Protein: 6g, Fat: 14g, Carbs: 10g, Sugar: 6g, Fiber: 3g, Sodium: 200mg

# Dessert and Soup Recipes

## 53.    Spinach and Feta Stuffed Mushrooms

- Time Required : 15 mins
- Curing time: 20 mins
- Serves: 4

Ingredients:

- 12 huge mushrooms, cleaned and stems removed
- 120g fresh spinach, hashed
- 75g feta cheese, crumbled
- 2 cloves garlic, hashed
- 30ml olive oil
- Salt and pepper to taste
- Fresh parsley

Directions:

1. Preheat oven to 180 degrees Celsius.
2. After washing, sauté the garlic and spinach in a little olive oil until the spinach wilts.
3. Once the pan is no longer hot, stir in the crumbled feta cheese.
4. Fill the mushroom caps with a little amount of the spinach and feta mixture.
5. Spread out a flat pan and arrange the filled mushrooms on top.

6. To get a soft texture, bake the mushrooms for around 15 to 20 mins.
7. Top each plate with a little freshly chopped parsley.

Nutrition Information: Kcals: 120, Protein: 6g, Fat: 9g, Carbs: 5g, Sugar: 2g, Fiber: 2g, Sodium: 180mg

## 54. Caprese Stuffed Avocado

- Time Required : 10 mins
- Curing time: 0 mins
- Serves: 2

Ingredients:

- 2 avocados, halved and pitted
- 150g cherry tomatoes, halved
- 125g fresh mozzarella balls
- Fresh basil leaves
- Balsamic glaze for drizzling
- Salt and pepper to taste

Directions:

1. To create space for the filling, slice a little piece of flesh from the middle of each avocado half.
2. Arrange fresh mozzarella balls, basil leaves, cherry tomatoes, and avocado on a single dish.
3. Use a small amount of the caprese mixture to fill the cavity of each avocado half.
4. After that, pour the balsamic glaze over the entire dish.
5. Before serving, season with a pinch of salt and pepper.
6. Serve right away when cooking is finished.

Nutrition Information: Kcals: 300, Protein: 8g, Fat: 25g, Carbs: 15g, Sugar: 5g, Fiber: 10g, Sodium: 100mg

## 55. Berry and Yogurt Parfait

- Time Required : 10 mins
- Assembly Time: 5 mins
- Serves: 2

Ingredients:

- 240g Greek yogurt
- 150g mixed berries strawberries, blueberries, raspberries
- 50g granola
- 30ml honey
- Mint leaves

Directions:

1. To make a parfait, layer two glasses with Greek yogurt, three glasses with mixed berries, and granola on top.
2. Perform the stacking procedure once again.
3. Drizzle honey on top.
4. For presentation, sprinkle over few mint leaves.
5. Serve right away when cooking is finished.

Nutrition Information: Kcals: 320, Protein: 20g, Fat: 10g, Carbs: 40g, Sugar: 20g, Fiber: 6g, Sodium: 80mg

## 56. Greek Yogurt and Berry Popsicles

- Time Required : 10 mins
- Freeze Time: 4 hours
- Makes: 6 popsicles

Ingredients:

- 480g Greek yogurt
- 150g mixed berries strawberries, blueberries, raspberries
- 30ml honey

- 5ml vanilla extract

Directions:

1. On a serving tray, mix together the Greek yogurt, fresh berries, honey, and vanilla essence.
2. With a spoon, transfer the mixture into the popsicle molds.
3. Popsicle sticks should be inserted into the center aperture of every mold.
4. To solidify, place in freezer for a minimum of four hours.
5. Just give the popsicles a short rinse in warm water to get them out of the molds.
6. Enjoy!

Nutrition Information: Kcals: 120, Protein: 8g, Fat: 4g, Carbs: 15g, Sugar: 10g, Fiber: 2g, Sodium: 30mg

## 57. Dark Chocolate and Berry Smoothie Dish

- Time Required : 10 mins
- Serves: 2

Ingredients:

- 2 frozen bananas
- 150g mixed berries strawberries, blueberries, raspberries
- 120ml almond milk
- 30g dark cocoa powder
- 15ml maple syrup
- Toppings: hashed strawberries, blueberries, granola, dark chocolate shavings

Directions:

1. Use a blender to combine frozen bananas, a variety of berries, almond milk, maple syrup, and dark chocolate powder. Proceed until there are no more bumps.
2. Process until a smooth and creamy consistency is achieved.
3. Divide the smoothie among the serving dishes.
4. Garnish with granola, strawberries, blueberries, and shavings of dark chocolate before serving.
5. Serve right away when cooking is finished.

Nutrition Information: Kcals: 250, Protein: 5g, Fat: 5g, Carbs: 50g, Sugar: 30g, Fiber: 8g, Sodium: 60mg

## 58. Sweet Potato and Kale Hash

- Time Required : 15 mins
- Curing time: 20 mins
- Serves: 2

Ingredients:

- 2 sweet potatoes, peeled and hashed
- 15ml olive oil
- 1 onion, hashed
- 60g kale, hashed
- 2 eggs, poached
- Salt and pepper to taste
- Paprika

Directions:

1. In a skillet set over medium heat, warm the olive oil.
2. When the sweet potatoes are browned and done, toss in the diced sweet potatoes and continue sautéing.
3. Toss in the chopped onion when it has loosened up in the pan.
4. Before cooking, toss the kale to coat it, and then let it wilt.
5. Divide the kale and sweet potato mixture among the plates.
6. Arrange a poached egg on each plate.
7. Before serving, season with a pinch of salt and pepper.
8. Before serving, sprinkle with a pinch of paprika.

Nutrition Information: Kcals: 320, Protein: 12g, Fat: 10g, Carbs: 45g, Sugar: 10g, Fiber: 8g, Sodium: 150mg

## 59.   Tomato and Basil Zoodle Salad

- Time Required : 10 mins
- Curing time: 0 mins
- Serves: 2

Ingredients:

- 2 zucchinis, spiralized into noodles
- 150g cherry tomatoes, halved
- 30g fresh basil, hashed
- 30ml balsamic glaze
- 15ml olive oil
- Salt and pepper to taste
- Parmesan cheese

Directions:

1. Slice some fresh basil, toss in some zucchini noodles, and top with cherry tomatoes (zoodles).
2. Olive oil and balsamic vinegar make a delicious glazing.
3. Just shake it slightly to coat.
4. Add a pinch of salt and freshly ground pepper right before serving.
5. Present it with a final dusting of grated Parmesan cheese.

Nutrition Information: Kcals: 180, Protein: 5g, Fat: 10g, Carbs: 20g, Sugar: 10g, Fiber: 5g, Sodium: 150mg

## 60.   Almond Flour Blueberry Muffins

- Time Required : 15 mins
- Cooking time: 25 mins
- Serving: 2 muffins

Ingredients:

- 80 grams almond flour

- 45 grams fresh blueberries
- 1 huge egg
- 15 grams erythritol or another sugar substitute 2.5 grams baking powder
- 2.5 grams vanilla extract

Directions:

1. Bake at 175 degrees Celsius. Get a muffin pan and line it with paper liners.
2. Baking powder, erythritol, and almond flour should be mixed in a basin.
3. Transfer the egg mixture to a separate dish and whisk in the vanilla extract.
4. At a slow but steady pace, incorporate the dry ingredients into the liquid mixture until a batter forms.
5. Add the blueberries and gently mix.
6. Half of the batter should go into each muffin pan liner.
7. A toothpick put into the middle of a muffin should emerge clean after 20 to 25 mins of baking.
8. After 10 mins, remove muffins from pan and allow to cool completely on a wire rack.

Nutritional Information: Kcals: 220 Protein: 9g Carbs: 10g Fiber: 5g Fat: 17g Sodium: 80mg

## 61. Strawberry Cheesecake Bites

- Time Required : 20 mins
- Freezing time: 1 hour
- Serving: 2

Ingredients:

- 4 huge strawberries
- 2 ounces cream cheese, softened
- 15 grams erythritol or another sugar substitute 2.5 grams vanilla extract
- 15 grams hashed nuts optional

Directions:

1. Remove the strawberry tops and use a regular spoon or knife to scoop out the fruit's insides. Remove from the heat.

79

2. Melt the cream cheese and mix in the erythritol and vanilla essence in a basin.
3. Make sure that every strawberry is filled with the cream cheese mixture.
4. If you'd like, you may top them with some hashed nuts.
5. Put the strawberries in the freezer for at least an hour, or until the cream cheese sets.
6. These nibbles are delicious either warm from the oven or eaten straight from the freezer.

Nutritional Information: Kcals: 110 Protein: 2g Carbs: 5g Fiber: 1g Fat: 9g Sodium: 75mg

## 62.    Almond Butter Cookies

- Time Required : 10 mins
- Cooking time: 12 mins
- Serving: 2

Ingredients:

- 125 grams almond flour
- 30 grams Stevia or another suitable sweetener 2.5 grams baking powder
- Pinch of salt
- 30 grams almond butter
- 5 grams coconut oil, melted
- 2.5 grams vanilla extract

Directions:

1. Preheat the oven to 175°C and line a baking sheet with parchment paper.
2. Gather all of the ingredients in a basin: almond flour, baking soda, Stevia, and salt.
3. Stir in the almond butter, vanilla essence, melted coconut oil, and dry ingredients. Combine all ingredients and mix until a dough forms.
4. Eight equal portions of dough should be formed. Form a ball using every component.
5. Pinch the balls together in your hands and press them lightly onto the prepared flat pan.
6. Ten to twelve mins in the oven should be enough time for a light golden brown hue to emerge around the edges.

7. After removing the cookies from the oven, let them to cool somewhat on the flat pan. Then, transfer them to a wire rack to cool completely.

Nutritional Information: Kcals: 210 Protein: 7g Carbs: 7g Fiber: 4g Fat: 17g Sodium: 90mg

## 63.  Cinnamon Roasted Almonds

- Time Required : 5 mins
- Cooking time: 15 mins
- Serving: 2

Ingredients:

- 125 grams raw almonds
- 15 grams olive oil
- 15 grams erythritol or another sugar substitute 5 grams cinnamon
- A pinch of salt

Directions:

1. Line a flat pan with parchment paper and set the oven to 175°C.
2. Mix the almonds with the olive oil, cinnamon, erythritol, and salt on a dish.
3. Arrange the almonds in a single layer on the prepared flat pan.
4. Toasted almonds with a nutty aroma will take around fifteen mins in the oven.
5. The almonds should be allowed to reach room temperature before being served.

Nutritional Information: Kcals: 305 Protein: 10g Carbs: 12g Fiber: 7g Fat: 27g Sodium: 75mg

## 64. Greek Yogurt with Mixed Berries

- Time Required : 5 mins
- Serving: 2

Ingredients:

- 125 grams unsweetened Greek yogurt
- 125 grams mixed berries strawberries, raspberries, blueberries 15 grams chia seeds
- 15 grams erythritol or another sugar substitute

Directions:

1. The Greek yogurt can be served by dividing it between two plates.
2. In the middle of each dish, place half of the mixed berries.
3. Split the erythritol and chia seeds evenly among the plates.
4. Gobble it up right away.

Nutritional Information: Kcals: 145 Protein: 14g Carbs: 16g Fiber: 5g Fat: 4g Sodium: 40mg

## 65. Sugar-Free Chocolate Avocado Mousse

- Time Required : 10 mins
- Cooling time: 1 hour
- Serving: 2

Ingredients:

- 1 ripe avocado
- 30 grams unsweetened cocoa powder
- 30 grams almond milk
- 30 grams erythritol or another sugar substitute 5 grams vanilla extract
- A pinch of salt

Directions:

1. Halve the avocado lengthwise to access the pit.
2. Toss the avocado flesh into a blender after spooning it out.

3. Melt the chocolate powder, almond milk, salt, vanilla extract, and erythritol in a blender. Proceed until there are no more bumps.
4. Combine all ingredients and whisk until smooth.
5. Put the two cups in the fridge for a minimum of an hour before you serve them.

Nutritional Information: Kcals: 170 Protein: 3g Carbs: 15g Fiber: 12g Fat: 15g Sodium: 75mg

# Exercise and Diabetes Management

In order to keep diabetes under control, frequent physical exercise is required. Maintaining a regular exercise routine is essential for people with diabetes and for improving their overall health and wellness. As we explore its complexities more, the advantages of this crucial component—which extend well beyond just being physically healthy—become more apparent.

## Importance of Physical Activity

When it comes to controlling diabetes, the significance of sticking to an exercise routine cannot be emphasized enough. When you exercise regularly, your body becomes more insulin sensitive, allowing it to better use the glucose it receives. This aids in glucose regulation and lessens the likelihood of insulin resistance, a common complication of diabetes.

With addition, being physically active may aid in weight maintenance, which is critical for diabetes management. Staying at a healthy weight lowers the risk of developing diabetes-related complications including cardiovascular disease, which improves blood sugar management.

Improvements in cardiovascular health should be prioritized for those with diabetes, since exercise plays a key role in accelerating this process. Essential components of comprehensive treatment for patients with diabetes include lowering the risk of heart disease, facilitating normal blood circulation, and facilitating blood pressure control.

## Tailoring Exercise to Individual Needs

Physical activity is good for everyone, but everyone requires a different approach to get the most out of it. A person's age, present fitness level, and general health should be considered while creating an exercise program. Because diabetes treatment is not a "one size fits all" situation, individualized plans are necessary.

A wide range of physical activities, such as aerobic exercise, flexibility training, and strength training, are recommended for people with diabetes. Cardiovascular health can be enhanced with aerobic workouts like cycling and brisk walking. Strength training, which includes resistance exercises, improves insulin sensitivity and muscle function. Yoga and other stretching exercises not only improve flexibility and overall health, but they may also help with stress management, an essential ability for those dealing with diabetes and its consequences.

## Overcoming Barriers to Exercise

Despite the clear benefits of regular physical activity, individuals with diabetes nevertheless encounter barriers that prohibit them from doing so. Typical obstacles include limited time, fear of hypoglycemia, and lack of desire. To conquer these challenges, a multi-pronged approach is necessary.

Incorporating regular physical activity into your routine is a smart choice. A few instances of this would include opting to swiftly walk a short distance instead of lounging on the couch and watching TV, or using the stairs instead of the elevator. One of the most important things you can do to be in shape is to surround yourself with supportive people. This can be in the form of a fitness club or even just your buddies. In addition, people with diabetes should consult with their doctors to develop individualized fitness plans that take into consideration their condition, goals, and any obstacles.

# Monitoring Blood Sugar Levels

Living a healthier lifestyle, including increasing physical exercise and monitoring blood sugar levels often, is essential for those with diabetes. Consistent monitoring allows individuals to make informed decisions regarding their lifestyle, medicines, and nutrition, leading to optimal glucose management.

## Self-Monitoring Techniques

Self-glycemic control The SMBG is a powerful tool in the battle against diabetes. By using SMBG, individuals may monitor their blood sugar levels throughout the day. In order to provide quick and precise results, modern glucometers just need a basic blood sample.

Knowing one's personal glucose patterns is essential for making educated judgments. By keeping tabs on their blood sugar levels on a regular basis, persons with diabetes may spot patterns, identify the factors influencing them, and make faster adjustments to their treatment plan.

## Understanding Blood Sugar Readings

A complete familiarity with target ranges and the factors influencing glycemic control is necessary for accurate interpretation of blood sugar results. The body's response to insulin the night before can be gleaned from fasting blood sugar levels, which are often measured first thing in the morning before meals. To learn how different foods affect blood sugar levels, it is helpful to take measurements after meals, or postprandial readings.

It may be required to make changes to medicine, exercise program, or food if blood sugar levels stay high for an extended period of time. However, difficulties might develop if hypoglycemia, a condition marked by low blood sugar, is not addressed promptly.

## Regular Check-ups and Medical Monitoring

Even while self-monitoring is key to controlling diabetes, a comprehensive treatment plan should also incorporate expert medical supervision and frequent check-ups. In order to assess a patient's overall health, identify any potential issues, and adjust treatment plans as necessary, medical experts play a crucial role.

Patients have thorough exams during their regularly scheduled checks, which could involve blood tests that provide a full assessment of their metabolic status. By doing these evaluations, we can find out how well the current management strategy is working and make any required adjustments.

Diabetic patients and healthcare providers must collaborate for the best possible outcome. Proactive diabetes management is promoted by keeping lines of communication open, which aids in the fast resolution of any new issues that may arise. One proactive and one reactive way to keep yourself healthy is to keep a record of your vitals on a regular basis.

# Medications and Insulin Management

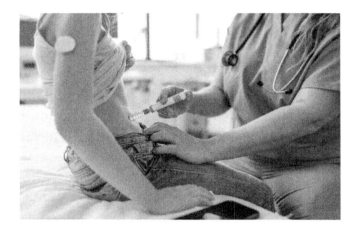

Patients with diabetes must take insulin and other medications in addition to engaging in regular physical exercise and monitoring their blood sugar levels in order to attain glycemic control. A thorough familiarity with the many prescription varieties, efficient insulin infusion techniques, and methods for controlling side effects is necessary for navigating the pharmaceutical landscape while treating patients with diabetes.

## Types of Diabetes Medications

A diverse array of medications, each with its own specific mechanism of action, comprise the pharmacological toolbox for the treatment and management of diabetes. Metformin and similar oral medications reduce glucose production by the liver and increase insulin sensitivity. Sulfonylureas aid diabetics in maintaining steady blood sugar levels by stimulating the pancreas to make more insulin.

Intravenous insulin release enhancers and glucagon secretaner inhibitors, such as GLP-1 receptor agonists and DPP-4 inhibitors, can improve glycemic control. An alternate group of oral medications called SGLT2 inhibitors aids in the body's improved glucose excretion via urine.

Insulin, a hormone essential for glucose metabolism, is a cornerstone of diabetes therapy. It is possible to tailor diabetes treatment programs to the unique needs of each patient by choosing from a variety of insulin formulations, including short-, intermediate-, and long-acting insulin.

## Insulin Administration and Monitoring

It is critical to give patients their insulin exactly as prescribed and at the exact times. Subcutaneous injections and insulin pumps are the two most common ways to provide insulin. Diabetics must acquire the necessary knowledge to ensure proper management and lessen the likelihood of complications.

ongoing monitoring of glucose levels The use of CGM devices has been a huge step forward in diabetes treatment technology. These techniques allow for the collection of data on blood sugar levels in real-time and the dynamic depiction of glycemic swings. Continuous glucose monitoring (CGM) devices enhance insulin regulation by facilitating the rapid adaptation to a variety of stimuli, such as dietary changes, exercise, and other variables.

## Managing Medication Side Effects

Diabetics should be mindful of the possible side effects of insulin and other medications, even if they assist achieve glycemic control. There are specific problems linked to each pharmaceutical group.

For example, some individuals have reported stomach issues when using metformin. It is important to monitor blood sugar levels often for sulfonylurea users since they may suffer hypoglycemia. Injection site responses can occur with injectable drugs, such as insulin, in certain individuals.

It is important for people to promptly inform their healthcare professionals of any concerns or negative side effects. Problems may be swiftly addressed by open communication, which allows for adjustments to medication regimens or the exploration of other choices.

There is more than just cutting calories out of your diet when it comes to treating diabetes. An all-encompassing treatment plan must include rigorous physical activity, meticulous monitoring of blood sugar levels, and cautious administration of medicines. People with diabetes can effectively manage their complex condition when they have a proactive strategy that is tailored to their specific needs. For some people, this means better glucose management and more general health.

# Conclusion

Our journey through the "Diabetic Cookbook" has begun, and it will change our lives in profound ways as we learn about diabetes management, nutrition, and overall wellness through the recipes included therein. An interesting look into the world of food is presented in this book. As you wind down your culinary journey, take a moment to think about what you've learned thus far and make mental notes of the key takeaways from the recipes, tips, and resources that have been presented.

Reading the "Diabetic Cookbook" is more than just perusing recipes and nutritional facts; it's a deliberate choice to take charge of your health, overcome the obstacles typically linked with diabetes, and live a fulfilling, balanced life. The goal of the "Diabetic Cookbook" is to help diabetics take back their health. When it comes to diabetic management, this cookbook is an excellent resource. In addition to recipes, it offers a philosophy—a way of eating with loved ones without sacrificing anything and experiencing life to the fullest.

Through her impressive culinary skills and extensive nutritional knowledge, the author eloquently argues that managing diabetes does not need sacrificing flavor or the excitement of cooking. It's a statement that the food you eat is a joyous occasion and a need, and that the kitchen is more of an art gallery than a battlefield. This expression is based on the principle that a kitchen is not the place for fighting. The central theme of this book is the possibility that living with diabetes may also be delicious, interesting, and rewarding. Being written by a diabetic qualifies it as a testimonial.

Chapters include a variety of topics related to diabetes management, such as the principles of diabetic nutrition and the intricacies of creating a balanced diabetic plate. Together, the sections on the essential kitchen tools and supplies, the subtle differences between sugar substitutes and the real deal, and the ins and outs of insulin and medicine administration give a comprehensive guide to navigating the complicated world of diabetes.

Now that its importance in promoting physical health and glycemic control has been better understood, exercise is seen as a potent tool in the battle against diabetes. This leads us to believe that physical activity is an effective strategy for diabetes management. The complexities of self-monitoring, the value of routine checkups, and blood sugar monitoring have all been clarified for you today. Navigating the ever-shifting landscape of your health will be a breeze with these newly acquired abilities.

An atypical diabetic cookbook has delivered on its promise: this culinary adventure has blossomed into a symphony of tastes, a hymn to nutritional knowledge, and a manual for choosing a lifestyle that is in tune with the difficulties of diabetes. The variety of foods provided, from breakfast staples to dessert treats, demonstrates that the promise was kept, since they are all prepared with care to ensure both flavor and nutritional harmony. Not only do people receive recipes, but they also receive the information they need to manage their diabetes effectively. This includes the capacity to understand the terminology around blood sugar levels, recipes, and a resource pack.

What we have here is a framework, not a rigid set of rules, that can adapt to the specific needs of each individual reader. It's a way of life that values the kitchen as a place of creativity, the plate as a work of art in the culinary arts, and every bite as an opportunity to savor the variety of human experience. Instead of being just a cookbook, this book is an invitation to self-feed as a kind of self-care, to rediscover the pleasure of cooking, and to savor the many different flavors.

This should be the one thing you take away from "The Diabetic Cookbook": The impact of eating on your emotional and physical health may cause you to rethink your current perspective. Diabetes management is more like a dance—you have to be the one to start it and the disease will follow suit—rather than a fixed state that requires constant attention. Enjoy the many tastes that life has to offer and be thankful for the chance to discover and create.

Put this book away, but instead of seeing it as the end of your culinary and health adventure, let it be the start of something exciting, rewarding, and totally original. More than just a cookbook, the "Diabetic Cookbook" is a health companion and guide to healthier eating and overall wellness. I wish you a voyage that is as satisfying and tasty as the recipes here. Wishing you a safe journey! A heartfelt greeting and a life well-lived are my wishes, regardless of my diabetes.

# Bonus Topic:

"The Art of Mindful Eating in Diabetes Management"

In the complicated treatment regimen for diabetes that involves diet, exercise, and medication, mindful eating is an essential but often ignored component. Beyond the food on one's plate and the limitations of conventional dietary norms, this supplementary chapter of the "Diabetic Cookbook" urges readers to embrace a holistic perspective.

The Crucial Component for Mindful Eating

Instead of focusing on calorie restriction, the core tenet of mindful eating is fostering a more deliberate and purposeful connection with food. It suggests that when taking care of one's body, one should savor each mouthful, engage all of one's senses, and live in the now. When dealing with the challenges of diabetes, practicing mindful eating may be a great assistance. It has the potential to lead to more self-awareness and improved management of blood sugar.

Taking pleasure in the present moment

A paradigm shift is possible via mindful eating in a culture where meals are more often than not hurriedly consumed, with little regard for them as opportunities for reflection and refueling. It is an implored slowdown, a separation from the chaos, and an embrace of the present moment. People with diabetes will benefit greatly from this shift in thinking. In its place, the often-stressed act of eating may be seen as a kind of self-care and self-love.

Pulling the Plug on Autopilot

Those of us who practice mindful eating should try to break free of the habit of letting our minds wander as we eat. It fights the urge to consume mindlessly, without giving any thought to the food we eat or why we eat it. Eating with purpose, rather than mindlessly, is essential for diabetes management. People may better meet their nutritional needs and work toward their health objectives when they have a firm grasp of the subtle distinctions between fullness and hunger.

Manage Your Blood Sugar Levels with Mindful Eating

Controlling blood sugar levels and practicing mindful eating go hand in hand. Those who take an active role in planning and preparing their meals have a greater chance of making choices that will reduce their blood sugar levels. Being aware of what goes into your food, how much you eat, and how different meals influence your blood sugar levels are all benefits of practicing mindful eating. With this newfound information, people may take a more active role in managing their diabetes by making educated dietary choices.

Purposeful Consumption and Its Pleasure Principle

Eating mindfully dispels the myth that diabetic-friendly food has to be bland and uninspiring and instead unlocks a world of delicious culinary possibilities. Savoring the distinct aromas, tastes, and textures of each dish is encouraged. Following the principles of mindful eating—which include not just providing the body with the nutrients it needs but also eating for genuine pleasure—is something the "Diabetic Cookbook" advocates for its readers. By shifting one's perspective, eating becomes an experience, not a chore, and a source of pleasure and fulfillment.

Setting Up Purposeful Routines in the Kitchen

When eating mindfully isn't happening in the dining room, it's in the kitchen, the heart of the house. "Diabetic Cookbook" is an ancillary topic that delves into the concept of mindful meal planning. It stresses the importance of being there as you chop, sauté, and combine ingredients, since this is when you can give each one a special role to play. Diabetics can get a sense of agency and creativity in the kitchen and a stronger connection to the act of self-sustenance via mindful cooking.

Mindful Emotion Consumption Management

Examining emotional eating from a mindfulness perspective is the focus of this supplementary subject. Having an emotional eater along on a diabetic's journey is not uncommon. Mindful eating helps with a lot of things, including learning to cope with emotions other than food, identifying emotional triggers, and telling the difference between emotional and physical hunger. It becomes a tool for resilience by offering an alternative to bad eating patterns that can help navigate the challenging emotional terrain.

Forging a Firm Connection Between Diet and Wellness

One of the main points of the "Diabetic Cookbook extra mindful" is the importance of developing a strong connection between what we eat and our overall health. It goes beyond dietary limitations and involves general health. Diabetes can be better managed if readers learn to include mindfulness principles into their culinary studies, which will lead them to basic linkages between diet and lifestyle. The opportunity of a lifetime may be right here. The act of eating becomes a joyous, nutritious, and empowering experience when one practices mindfulness as they move from fork to plate.

Printed in Great Britain
by Amazon